THE LIFE OF MOHAMMED

THE SIRA

BILL WARNER, PHD

CENTER FOR THE STUDY OF
POLITICAL ISLAM

THE LIFE OF MOHAMMED

THE SIRA

BILL WARNER, PHD

CENTER FOR THE STUDY OF
POLITICAL ISLAM

ISBN13 978-1-936659-06-7
PUBLISHED BY CSPI, LLC

This book is dedicated to the
millions of victims of jihad over the last 1,400 years.
May you read this and become a voice for the voiceless.

TABLE OF CONTENTS

TO THE READER

After the attack on the World Trade Towers on September 11, 2001, I realized that I lived in a world where almost no one knew the doctrine of Islam. My study of Islam had started back in the '70's, so I decided that I would devote my life to educating the world about its political doctrine. Once you understand the doctrine, you will understand history and what is to come.

Few people understand Islam because its doctrine is based on the Trilogy of texts—the Koran, the Sira (the biography of Mohammed), and Hadith (his traditions)—which are written in an obscure manner. This book gives the reader a simple way to understand Islamic doctrine.

The method used in this book for understanding Islamic doctrine is:
- You study Islamic political doctrine, not religion or Muslims.
- The writing is simple and straightforward.
- Learning takes place in stages and through repetition.
- This book is from the perspective of the non-Muslim, so the religion is of no importance.
- This book contains objective knowledge, not opinion. All references can be read and verified by using the reference number that precedes paragraphs.
- This book is based on fact-based reasoning.

A common dismissal of Islamic doctrine is that moderate Muslims do not follow it. This book is not about Muslims, moderate or extreme, but about Islamic political doctrine and history.

You will only get a personal point of view when you ask a Muslim about Islam. And what kind of Muslim do you ask, moderate or jihadi? Both moderate Muslims and jihadis all submit to the Sunna of Mohammed and the Koran.

We are fortunate to live in a time when the doctrine of Islam has been made simple. Islam is a fascinating subject—enjoy your read.

Bill Warner, Ph.D.

PREFACE

THE CSPI TEACHING METHOD

Everything you say about political Islam has to reference the Islamic foundational texts found in the Trilogy: Koran, Sira, Hadith.

The CSPI Teaching Method is the easiest and quickest way to learn about Islam.

Authoritative

There are only two ultimate authorities about Islam—Allah and Mohammed. Allah is found in the Koran. Mohammed is found in the Sira (Mohammed's biography) and in the Hadith (his words and actions). CSPI approaches these three Islamic texts from the point of view of the Kafir (non-Muslim). A referencing system allows the reader to verify the book content from the Islamic foundational source texts.

Systemic Knowledge

The easiest way to study Islam is to see the whole picture. For instance, the Koran alone cannot be understood due to a lack of context, but when the life of Mohammed is added, it makes sense.

Levels of Learning

The ideas of Islam are very foreign to our civilization. It takes repetition to grasp the new ideas. The CSPI method uses four levels of training to teach the doctrine in depth. The first level is designed for a beginner and lays out the entire scope of Islam. Each level and book repeats the basics to insure in depth learning. Therefore each book can be read on its own or as part of the full series.

Political Islam, Not Religious Islam

Islam has a political doctrine and a religious doctrine. Its political doctrine concerns everyone, while religious Islam only concerns Muslims. CSPI books deal only with political Islam and Mohammed, not Muslims.

Scientific Approach

The CSPI method employs a rational or scientific approach with fact-based reasoning to study the Islamic doctrine. CSPI uses simple statistics, graphs and categorization to analyze the doctrine. We do not question the truth of the doctrine, we merely examine objectively what is there. We hold this truth to be self evident: Koran + Sira + Hadith (Trilogy) = Islamic Doctrine. To uphold the truth of the doctrine, CSPI stresses the importance of precise naming when discussing political Islam.

LEVEL 1—INTRODUCTION TO POLITICAL ISLAM AND SHARIA

A Self-Study Course on Political Islam - Level 1., Sharia Law for Non-Muslims; The Life of Mohammed - The Sira; The Hadith - The Sunna of Mohammed; A Two Hour Koran

LEVEL 2—APPLIED DOCTRINE, SPECIAL TOPICS

A Self-Study Course on Political Islam - Level 2., Factual Persuasion - Changing the Minds of Islam's Supporters; The Islamic Doctrine of Women; The Islamic Doctrine of Christians and Jews; The Doctrine of Slavery - An Islamic Institution; An Abridged Koran - Readable and Understandable.

See also an adapted reprint from 1924 of Andre Savier: *Islam and the Psychology of the Muslim.*

LEVEL 3—INTERMEDIATE TRILOGY

A Self-Study Course on Political Islam - Level 3., Mohammed and the Unbelievers—The Sira, a Political Biography; The Political Traditions of Mohammed—The Hadith for the Unbelievers; Simple Koran—The Reconstructed Historical Koran.

See also an adapted reprint from 1901 of Rev. W. St.Clair-Tisdall: *The Sources of Islam—A Persian Treatise* (translated by Sir William Muir) published by CSPI.

LEVEL 4—ORIGINAL SOURCE TEXTS

SIRA: *Sirat Rasul Allah* by Ibn Ishaq (704-770 AD) in A. Guillaume: *The Life of Muhammad* (first English edition in 1955).

History of the Prophets and Kings by Muhammad ibn Jarir al-Tabari (839-923 AD), (first English edition in 1879).

The Life of Mohammad by Sir William Muir (first English edition in 1863).

HADITH: Sahih Bukhari 9 volumes, Sahih Muslim 7 volumes, Sunan Abu Dawood 5 volumes.

KORAN: Ali, Maulana Muhammad. *Holy Koran.* Columbus, Ohio: Ahmadiyyah Anjuman Ishaat Islam, 1998.

Arberry, A. J. *The Koran Interpreted,* NY: Touchstone, 1996.

Dawood, N. J. *The Koran,* London: Penguin Books, 1999.

Pickthall, Mohammed M. *The Meaning of the Glorious Koran.* Kuwait: Dar al-Islamiyya.

SHARIA: *Reliance of the Traveller and Tools of the Worshipper—The Classic Manual of Islamic Sacred Law,* original title "'Umdat as-Salik wa 'Uddat an-Nasik," by Ahmad ibn Naqib al-Misri (1302-1367 AD), edited and translated by Nu Ha Mim Keller.

MAP OF
ARABiA
600 A.D.

BLACK SEA

ANATOLIA
[TURKEY]

CASPIAN
SEA

MEDITERRANEAN
SEA

[SYRIA]

PERSIA
[IRAN]

MESOPOTAMIA
[IRAQ]

•Muta

•Tabuk

•Fadak
•Khaybar

ARABIA

•Medina
•Badr

[EGYPT]

RED SEA

•Mecca
•Hudabiya
•Hunain

AFRICA

YEMEN

N

ABYSSINIA
[ETHIOPIA]

INTRODUCTION

CHAPTER 1

Up until now the study of Islamic doctrine has been by Arab language scholars, historians, theologians and students of Middle East culture. Critical thought has been used, but there has never been a fully scientific approach to Islamic doctrine.

There have been two things that you have been told about Islam that are not true. The first is that it is only a religion. This is the most common misconception. Generally speaking, those who maintain that Islam is just a religion are non-Muslims, because most Muslims insist on the fact that Islam is a complete philosophy, a complete way of life that includes religion but also politics, culture and everything else it takes to run a civilization.

The second error is that Islam is nearly impossible to understand or at the very least that it takes a great deal of lengthy study in school, preferably college.

THE SCIENTIFIC METHOD

The CSPI books utilize a scientific approach in order to get results that go beyond opinion, because if we're going to speak about Islam we need to have more than opinion. We have enough of that already. We need a fact-based approach, something that makes sense and is coherent. We also need an explanation that is systematic and shows us the entire story of Islam in a straightforward manner.

If we try to sort out the different opinions about Islam, and we look to a professional or an expert, exactly which expert do we turn to? If we're going to ask a Muslim, do we ask someone who is nice or do we ask a jihadist, because both of them claim to be Muslims? Do we ask a college professor, someone in the media, a Muslim at work or do we go to the internet? Because when we go to the internet there is a riot of opinions on Islam. So how do you sort it out? Where do we find factual information?

The study of Islam is also obscured by political correctness. Criticism of Islam is frequently called bigotry because anything that is said that offends Muslims is considered racism or bigotry. This political correctness shuts off any real debate because if someone says something that a Muslim finds offensive then how are we ever to discuss anything that is negative about Islam? There are negative aspects to all thought systems and all philosophies.

We have to be able to move beyond the fact that critical thought is called bigoted thought.

What is the true nature of Islam? We will not find out the true nature of Islam by media comments or other informal methods.

To do this we will have to find a way to discuss Islam that is fact-based, scientific and provable, one that goes beyond opinion. If something is objective or scientific, it means that no matter who does the work, they will come up with the same results. We must have an objective way to study Islam in which everybody gets the same answer.

Using the scientific approach is going to let us be absolutely authoritative. We're going to be able to state things about Islam and we're going to know that we are right, that this is not just an opinion, but that it has substance to it and facts behind it.

Part of the scientific method is precisely defined names and terms. What we see today are words that are vague and subjective. What is a extremist Muslim? The name extremist Muslim is not found anywhere in Islamic doctrine. The CSPI method is to use names and terms that are based on the doctrine.

THE STARTING POINT

If we're going to have a scientific analysis of Islam, we have to have a foundation that is unassailable, because if we start off from a questionable assumption everything after that can be challenged.

There is a place in the study of Islam that is absolutely sure and certain. There's a point at which we can start, that every Muslim from the past, the present and the future all agree on without a single exception. That is the statement:

> There is no god but Allah and Mohammed is his messenger.

This declaration of Mohammed and Allah is called the *shahada* and if said in Arabic in front of witnesses, means that you are now a practicing Muslim. But, this statement about Mohammed and Allah is not just the beginning of Islam but also the very foundation and even the totality of Islam.

How can such a small statement contain all of Islam? It talks about Mohammed and about Allah. And it turns out that all of Islam, without any exception, is based upon Allah and Mohammed.

There is no god but Allah. Now where will we learn about Allah? Well, that would come from the Koran, which seems a difficult place to start because the Koran seems to be so little understood. But as we will see, the

Koran can actually be quite easily understood and we can understand the true nature of Allah after we know who Mohammed is.

THE TWO KORANS

Let's examine the Koran. Frequently, it is a big thick green book that contains both English and Arabic. When we try to read it, it's quite puzzling. First of all, there doesn't seem to be any time in the Koran. When we turn a page we don't go forward in time, we could go backwards or perhaps we're not even sure if time has moved at all. It also seems chaotic. One subject follows another in seemingly random fashion.

Then we come to contradictions. We'll read one verse in the Koran which seems kind:

Koran 109:6 *You shall have your religion and I shall have my religion.*

But there are other passages in the Koran which are very violent: cutting off hands and feet, crucifixions, and torture:

Koran 9:5 *When the sacred months are over slay the idolaters wherever you find them. Arrest them, besiege them, and lie in ambush everywhere for them. If they repent and take to prayer and render the alms levy, allow them to go their way. God is forgiving and merciful.*

This violent material contained within the Koran produces a contradiction. Is the Koran about good or is the Koran about violence?

There are actually two different Korans in the same book. There is an early Koran from Mecca and a later Koran from Medina. And those two contrast greatly, and frequently they contradict each other. The first Koran, written in Mecca, is quite religious and the second, or later Koran written in Medina, is very political. This corresponds to Mohammed's career. First he was a religious preacher, then he became a politician and jihadist. There's such a strong contrast between them that we're left with an uncertainty of what the Koran's true nature is. But everything that appears to be a contradiction is actually a key to understanding the true nature of Islam.

Another confusing aspect about the Koran is that there doesn't seem to be enough information in it. Most people have heard of the Five Pillars of Islam: the declaration of Allah and Mohammed, the charity tax, fasting during Ramadan, the pilgrimage to Mecca and praying five times a day.

But when you read the Koran carefully, none of these Five Pillars is explained and yet every Muslim seems to know how to do them. How is this? We will see that there's a big piece missing from the Koran, and that missing piece is Mohammed.

3

PUTTING MOHAMMED BACK INTO THE KORAN

It turns out that scholars since the days of Mohammed have known the proper order of the chapters in the Koran. So the first step towards understanding the Koran and making it readable is simply to put everything in the right time order. The other important step is to group similar topics together. For instance the story of Moses occurs again and again. And if we group all those stories about Moses together they become quite easy to understand.

But the main technique that makes the Koran readable is to bring Mohammed into the picture. Now this is not a novel suggestion. Any book written by Muslim scholars that is about the interpretation of the Koran always brings Mohammed into the picture. Mohammed gives us the context that we need to understand the Koran.

When we put the chapters in the right time order, group similar topics and then introduce Mohammed, we wind up with an easily understood epic story. It starts off with a hymn to God and ends in political triumph over all peoples.

The importance of Mohammed is clearly given to us in the Koran itself. There are over 90 verses which say Mohammed is the perfect Muslim. Every Muslim is to imitate Mohammed in every way and in every detail of his life. It goes on further to say that those who do not imitate Mohammed will go to hell. So Mohammed is the key to understanding the Koran and Islam.

We know a great deal about Mohammed because there are two books that give us all the information about him. The first is a book called the Sira. The word sira means biography. Usually when it's a capital "S," it refers to the biography of Mohammed. We have an extensive biography of Mohammed which runs about 800 pages in fine print. We know an enormous amount about his life.

The second book is comprised of the Hadith, traditions, short stories, about Mohammed. The shortest tradition is three words – "War is deceit." But there are other traditions telling us what Mohammed did, how he drank a glass of water, how he put on his shoes, or what judgment he gave about a certain person.

So we have two sets of foundational texts that give us Mohammed: the Sira and the Hadith.

THE ISLAMIC BIBLE—THE TRILOGY

Islam is defined by the words of Allah in the Koran, and the words and actions of Mohammed, the Sunna.

So the Trilogy is the Koran, the Sira and the Hadith. Most people think that the Koran is the "bible" of Islam, but it is only about 14% of the total textual doctrine. The Trilogy is the foundation and totality of Islam.

RELATIVE SIZES OF TRILOGY TEXTS

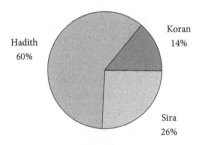

Hadith
60%

Koran
14%

Sira
26%

RELATIONSHIP BETWEEN SUNNA AND KORAN

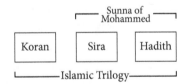

KAFIR

The first step in learning about Islam is to know the right definition of words. The language of Islam is dualistic. There is a division of humanity into believer and non-believer, kafir. Humanity is divided into those who believe Mohammed is the prophet of Allah, and those who do not.

Kafir is the actual word the Koran uses for non-Muslims. It is usually translated as unbeliever, but that translation is wrong. The word unbeliever is neutral. As you will see, the attitude of the Koran towards unbelievers is very negative. The Koran defines the Kafir in the following ways:

The Kafir is hated—

Koran 40:35 *They [Kafirs] who dispute the signs [Koran verses] of Allah without authority having reached them are greatly hated by Allah and the believers. So Allah seals up every arrogant, disdainful heart.*

A Kafir can be beheaded—

Koran 47:4 *When you encounter the Kafirs on the battlefield, cut off their heads until you have thoroughly defeated them and then take the prisoners and tie them up firmly.*

A Kafir can be plotted against—

Koran 86:15 *They plot and scheme against you [Mohammed], and I plot and scheme against them. Therefore, deal calmly with the Kafirs and leave them alone for a while.*

A Kafir can be terrorized—

Koran 8:12 *Then your Lord spoke to His angels and said, "I will be with you. Give strength to the believers. I will send terror into the Kafirs' hearts, cut off their heads and even the tips of their fingers!"*

A Kafir can be made war on and humiliated—

Koran 9:29 *Make war on those who have received the Scriptures [Jews and Christians] but do not believe in Allah or in the Last Day. They do not forbid what Allah and His Messenger have forbidden. The Christians and Jews do not follow the religion of truth until they submit and pay the poll tax [jizya], and they are humiliated.*

A Muslim is not the friend of a Kafir—

Koran 3:28 *Believers should not take Kafirs as friends in preference to other believers. Those who do this will have none of Allah's protection and will only have themselves as guards. Allah warns you to fear Him for all will return to Him.*

In Islam, Christians and Jews are infidels and "People of the Book"; Hindus are polytheists and pagans. The terms infidel, People of the Book, pagan and polytheist are religious words. Only the word "Kafir" shows the common political treatment of the Christian, Jew, Hindu, Buddhist, animist, atheist and humanist. What is done to a pagan can be done to a Christian, atheist or any other Kafir.

The word Kafir will be used in this book instead of "unbeliever", "non-Muslim" or "disbeliever". Unbeliever or non-Muslim are neutral terms, but Kafir is not a neutral word. Instead, it defines a subhuman, so it is bigoted and biased. Kafir is capitalized since Muslim is capitalized.

It is astounding how much of Islamic doctrine is about the Kafir. Over half, 51%, is about the Kafir.

AMOUNT OF TEXT DEVOTED TO THE KAFIR

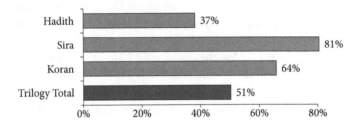

THE THREE VIEWS OF ISLAM

There are three points of view in dealing with Islam. The point of view depends upon what you believe about Mohammed. If you believe Mohammed is the prophet of Allah, then you are a believer. If you don't believe this, you are a *Kafir*. The third viewpoint is that of an apologist for Islam.

Apologists do not believe that Mohammed was a prophet, but they never say anything that would displease a Muslim. They never offend Islam and condemn any analysis that is critical of Islam as being biased.

Let us give an example of the three points of view.

Kab bin al-Ashraf wrote poems that Mohammed said harmed Allah and himself. Mohammed got a Muslim to deceive and assassinate Kab.

- Muslims view this death as necessary because Kab harmed Mohammed and Allah.
- Kafirs look at this event as proof of the jihadic violence of Islam and as an evil act.
- Apologists say that this was a historic event, that all cultures have violence in their past, and that no judgment should be passed.

According to the different points of view, assassinating Kab was either evil, a perfect godly act or only another historical event, take your pick.

This book is written from the Kafir point of view and is therefore, Kafir-centric. Everything in this book views Islam from how it affects Kafirs, non-Muslims. This also means that the religion is of little importance. Only a Muslim cares about the religion of Islam, but all Kafirs are affected by Islam's political views.

Notice that there is no right and wrong here, merely different points of view that cannot be reconciled. There is no possible resolution between the view of the Kafir and the Muslim. The apologist tries to bring about a bridge building compromise, but it is not logically possible.

THE CSPI DOCTRINAL METHOD

The actions and words of Muslims have their foundation in the doctrine of Islam found in the Islamic Trilogy of the Koran, Sira and Hadith. This doctrine must be analyzed and understood on a rational basis and on its own merits. When you know the doctrine of Islam, then you can understand every action by Muslims, and reasonably predict future behavior.

The doctrinal method is fact-based and scientific. It posits a cause and effect relationship between Islamic doctrine and the behavior and speech of Muslims. If an opinion or comment about Islam does not have a reference, or a possible reference, to the Trilogy, then the opinion has little merit.

The CSPI doctrinal method examines Islamic history and current events as being the fruit of its doctrine. Since both past and present Islam are based upon the same unchanging doctrine, it is possible to understand from the actions of Muslims today and what the future will bring.

SUMMARY

There is a scientific, objective way to study Islam. It does not depend on opinion. It depends on three texts – the Islamic bible, the Trilogy. Everything about Islam is explained by those three texts so there's no need for opinion. There's no need to go and ask someone else. Islam is based on the Sunna of Mohammed, his words and deeds as recorded in the Sira and Hadith. If you know what Mohammed did, if you know his perfect pattern of life, then you don't need to ask a Muslim what a Muslim should do.

It also means that if you're ever discussing Islam, as long as you're basing your points on the example of Mohammed, then you are correct no matter whom you're dealing with, even if it's an Arabic scholar or an imam. Because once you know Mohammed, you know Islam. You have taken your information from the Koran, the Sira, the Hadith and there is no higher authority and there is no deeper knowledge.

The use of fact-based knowledge takes us away from the emotional world and the fear of being called a bigot, the fear of displeasing someone. We go to the realm of the mind and deal with facts. We can deal with the Koran and the Sunna. There's no bigotry in numbers nor is there Islamophobia when you are quoting Mohammed.

When you finish reading the CSPI Koran, Sira and Hadith you will be able to reason and argue in a way that goes beyond anything that you've thought possible before. You will become logical and fact-based in your reasoning and will become powerful in persuading others.

THE REFERENCE SYSTEM

Everything in CSPI books and charts is verifiable. If you do not agree with, want to learn more, or want to confirm what is written, refer to the noted source. The first letter of the author's last name indicates the source text. Reference numbers are provided allowing you to look it up in the source text. It is similar to a chapter/verse. Examples below:

HADITH

(B) *Sahih al-Bukhari* by Muhammad al-Bukhari
Example: B 1,3,4 is *Sahih al-Bukhari*, volume 1, book 3, number 4
(M) *Sahih Muslim* by Muslim ibn al-Hajjaj
Example: M012,1234 is *Sahih Muslim*, book 12, number 1234
(T) *The History of al-Tabari* by the State University of New York is a translation of *History of Prophet and Kings* by Muhammad ibn Jarir al-Tabari
Example: T11921 is *The History of al-Tabari*, margin note 11921

SIRA

(I) *The Life of Muhammad* by Ibn Ishaq, translated by A. Guillaume
Example: I125 is *The Life of Muhammed*, number printed in the margin
(T) *The History of al-Tabari* by the State University of New York is a translation of *History of Prophet and Kings* by Muhammad ibn Jarir al-Tabari
Example: T11921 is *The History of al-Tabari*, margin note 11921
(WM) *The Life of Muhammad* by W. Muir
Example: WM123 is *The Life of Muhammed*, page 123

KORAN

(Koran) Multiple. See "Translating the Koran into English" for a list by author.
Koran 2:123 is a reference to the Koran, chapter (sura) 2, verse 123

SHARIA LAW

(RT) *The Reliance of the Traveller,* by Shihabuddin Abu al-'Abbas Ahmad ibn an-Naqib al-Misri
Example: RT 08.2

SPELLING

It is the present state of knowledge of the West about Islam that there is no standardized spelling of proper Arabic nouns. Examples: Muslim/Moslem, Mohammed/Muhammad, Koran/Quran, kaffir/kafir.

A GUIDE TO THE SIRA

Reading the Sira, Mohammed's biography, is the first step towards objective knowledge about Islam. Knowing the Sira moves the discussion away from opinions. It is a foundational approach; you don't need an expert once you know Mohammed, the supreme expert.

We are going to view Mohammed from the standpoint of the Kafir, the nonbeliever. When you read the Sira it is very much about the world from the standpoint of Islam because every time a Kafir suffers or dies or loses, the Sira is triumphant. The Kafir is evil and his destruction and suffering are good.

The word "sira" means biography in Arabic but the Sira with a capital "S" means the biography of Mohammed. The analysis we will use is our first step to learning about the Sunna, the words and deeds of Mohammed as recounted in the Sira and Hadith. It's the perfect path, the perfect example of Mohammed, the perfect Muslim. If a Muslim is to copy Mohammed in everything that they do or say then, they need to know what Mohammed did and said. The Sira, his biography, gives us that.

Mohammedanism describes Islam. A Muslim is not someone who worships Allah. A Muslim is one who worships Allah in the exact manner that Mohammed did. This means the exact way, not close, not similar, but 100% like Mohammed.

Since the Koran does not give enough information to practice Islam, it turns out that every Muslim's life is based primarily on the perfect example of Mohammed. To understand Mohammed we need to start with the biography. He establishes the pattern of Islam, the direction of Islam, the progression of Islam, because every Muslim is to duplicate him.

When people want to learn about Islam, their first instinct is to try to read the Koran. Most people don't finish reading it and do not understand it. Oddly enough, this confusion frequently passes for profoundness. The right place you want to start to learn Islam is with Mohammed. Once you understand Mohammed, the Koran becomes quite easy to comprehend. The converse is true as well. If you do not understand Mohammed, you will never understand the Koran.

As a matter of fact, you cannot understand the Koran at all without Mohammed. If you open a scholar's text on the Koran, you will soon discover that Mohammed is what gives the context to all the verses in the Koran.

Any comments about the Koran always have to involve Mohammed in some way. If you don't know Mohammed when you try reading the Koran, there's a deep background story that you don't have. You don't have a point of reference. You also don't have any sense of the progression in Islam. How Islam changes is one of the important things you're going to understand by learning about the *Sira*. You will understand that Islam is a process that starts one way and ends another. It has two distinct phases, but for you o understand those phases, you must understand the life of Mohammed.

The reason we can't understand the Koran that we get in the bookstore is that Mohammed has been removed. When you put Mohammed into the Koran it is easy to understand. This is what CSPI books do for you.

The great advantage of a story is that it is very easy to remember. Facts are hard to remember, but you do not forget a story. So the Sira is the easiest part of learning about Islam. It's an amazing story that you will never forget.

We need to know that we study the most authoritative biography, the one that cannot be challenged. We will use *The Life of Muhammad*,[1] by Ibn Ishaq, the oldest and most authoritative biography.

Ishaq is the supreme standard for the life of Mohammed. No professor, no imam, no cleric, can give you a deeper and more basic knowledge about Islam and Mohammed than the Sira by Ishaq, the final authority.

HOW TO READ THE SIRA

When you read the Sira, you need to know that it is much more than a biography. On one level it can be read as one of the great biographies of history. Mohammed goes from being an orphan to the first ruler of all of Arabia. But it is much more than a biography; it is a sacred text, similar to the Gospels of the New Testament.

Below are three of over 90 Koran verses that point to the need to pattern your life on the example of Mohammed:

Koran 61:10 *Believers! Should I show you a profitable exchange that will keep you from severe torment? Believe in Allah and His messenger and fight valiantly for Allah's cause [jihad] with both your wealth and your lives.*

58:5 *Those who oppose Allah and His Messenger will be laid low, just as those who came before them.*

3:31 *Say: Obey Allah and His messenger, but if they reject it, then truly, Allah does not love those who reject the faith.*

---

1 Ibn Ishaq, *The Life of Muhammad*, translated by A. Guillaume (Karachi: Oxford University Press, 1982).

Mohammed is the ideal pattern for how to live the perfect Islamic life. He is beloved and cannot be criticized. He is perfect in every way. Every Muslim is to repeat his life, down to the smallest detail—how to drink water, how to put on shoes, or even how to use the bathroom. Every Muslim is supposed to be a Mohammedan.

Mohammed is revered. There are jokes about Jesus, Noah, St. Peter, God, but there are no jokes about Mohammed. He may have laughed at others, but no one, Muslim or Kafir, had better joke about Mohammed. In present times men have been killed and city blocks destroyed because of a cartoon about Mohammed. Sharia (Islamic law) has the death penalty for the blasphemy of Mohammed.

Another way to read the Sira is to see it as a manual of how Islam progressively enters a society. Islam enters a culture as a religion. Everything is fine between Muslims and the new host nation. It comes into a culture at first in a very soft, almost sweet manner, just like any other religion. Indeed, in the very first part of its societal growth, Islam is hardly distinguishable from a religion like Christianity. But as soon as it begins to gather any strength Islam changes and starts to put pressure on the host culture, to make demands. And these demands against the culture are relentless, ongoing and forever. Islam is always right and the host culture is always completely wrong. Everything about Islam is perfect and everything about the host culture must be changed.

Then when Islam gains enough strength, the violence starts. At first the violence is merely in the form of threats. Then the violence is against individuals in the form of assassinations, following the example of Mohammed who frequently executed his intellectual enemies and political and military opponents. Violence is also used to gain money and that money is put towards jihad. It does not stop until the host country is 100% Islamic. To see how this works, look at North Africa, Turkey, Iraq and so on. These areas were once Christian, but today they are 90 - 100% Islamic. It may take centuries, but ultimately, a nation will become completely Islamic.

Today, the Kafir nations that border Islam suffer violence. These bloody borders of Islam are a manifestation of Mohammed. He attacked every single neighbor without exception. He made war against pagans, Jews and Christians.

As soon as Mohammed had conquered his nearest neighbors, the Jews and polytheists, he turned north to the Christian world in Syria. If he had lived longer, then the Koran would have been filled with war against the Christian world. As it turned out, the job of crushing the Christians of the

Middle East was left to Umar, the second caliph. A caliph is Allah's vice regent on earth and is similar to a pope/political/military leader.

Mohammed was never satisfied as long as there was one person left in his life who was not a Muslim. Every aspect of society had to yield to his will. Islam is never satisfied until the country is Islamic. Ironically, this is carried out at the same time Muslims are declaring that Islam is tolerant towards all religion.

THE DIFFICULTY OF THE SIRA

If you pick up the original Sira that was been translated into English, it's about 800 pages in fine print. It is written in difficult academic prose. One paragraph can be a page and a half long. There is one chapter that's nothing but names. There are other chapters which include great lists of names of those who participated in events. And then there is the difficulty of the long Arabic names themselves.

Another difficulty of the book is that when you get through reading it, you discover there's another 100 pages left that are technical details which add to the confusion.

Another surprise to western readers is how much poetry is in this Sira. Indeed, about 25% of the text is poetry. But it's poetry of a most peculiar sort. It's always about "thumping your chest" and insulting your enemies and how you and your allies are powerful, brave heroes. It's war poetry, pure and simple. Here is an example:

My mother's son blames me because if I were ordered to kill him I would strike his neck with a sharp sword.

A blade white as salt from polishing.

My downward stroke never misses its mark.

It would not please me to kill you voluntarily though we owned all of Arabia from north to south.

This type of poetry goes on for page after page. Heroic war poetry taunts the enemy and praises heroes but it does not advance the plot or the story. You learn nothing about Mohammed. The poetry is entertaining perhaps, but it is not informative. The poetry is useful for some advanced scholarship but it is not needed for our purposes of learning the life of Mohammed. Hence, it is not included in the condensed books use here.

There's a matter of miracles that are found in the Sira. Now these miracles don't take up much space but they need to be pruned. The Sira reports that one of the taunts of his fellow citizens was that if Mohammed was working for Allah why couldn't he perform a miracle and prove his divine authority. The Sira further records that Mohammed's answer was that he was only a messenger, not a miracle worker. So the Sira both says that Mohammed could not do miracles and it says that he did miracles. The Koran however, is insistent upon the fact that Mohammed was only a messenger, not a miracle worker. We follow the Koran and do not include miracles in the Sira.

Then there are some Arab names that give the English reader some pause because they are very long. If you have a good understanding of Arabic, those names won't slow you down, but for the ordinary English reader it is almost impossible to keep up with the plot.

An Arab name in the Sira is long because it includes his ancestry, his lineage. The cultural barrier is a large one for the first-time reader and so in the Sira that has been prepared for you a one-word name is used. For instance, a person who appears frequently within the Sira is Umar bin al Katab. We just call him Umar. And if a person does not play a large role, he is named strictly by his function. For instance Abdullah bin Atik is called one of Salam's assassins.

Then there are the 109 pages of technical endnotes. The original text has long since vanished and the man who gave us this copy of Ishaq added his own notes at the end. Again, these are useful to a scholar but they don't advance the plot nor do they give us any needed information about Mohammed. Here's an example, endnote 287:

> Some say that Uamir was the son of Amir or of Zayid.

Interesting perhaps for a Ph.D. thesis, but it does not add to our knowledge of Islam.

So the book that you will be reading has eliminated almost all the poetry and lists of names and simplified the long, Arabic names. And the academic prose has been rewritten into standard, readable English.

IN THE BEGINNING

CHAPTER 3

*This [Allah cast terror into the Kafir's heart] was because they
opposed Allah and His messenger. Ones who oppose Allah and His
messenger will be severely punished by Allah.* [Koran 8:13]

Mohammed did not create the doctrine of Islam out of thin air or as a philosophical exercise. Each verse and hadith is a response to events in Mohammed's life. In short, there is a context and that context comes from the Sira, Mohammed's biography.

In the Hadith (the traditions of Mohammed) we see the small details, but no big picture. The Koran has almost no story and very little reference to any history. The Sira provides a compelling vision of Mohammed and the explosion of Islam. Only the Sira gives an explanation of how Islam and its doctrine are a historical development.

Mohammed went from being a preacher to a politician and warrior. As a preacher he garnered only 150 followers in 13 years. Then he changed Islam's strategy into a political form. After 10 years of jihad—holy war— Mohammed became the first ruler of all of Arabia and he did not have a single opponent left alive in Arabia. He was completely and totally politically triumphant. The process required 9 years of effort with a violent event every 7 weeks.

The Sira is primarily about jihad. Over 75% of the text is about a political struggle, raids, battles and theft. It is jihad that produces slavery and the political basis for the legal subjugation of women.

The Sira gives a context to Islam. Without the Sira and the Hadith, there is no Islam. Without the story of Mohammed, the Koran is incomprehensible and meaningless.

The paragraphs of the Sira that relate to women have this symbol in the margin. ♀

If the paragraph is about slaves there is this symbol in the margin. §

And if it relates to a female slave or women and slavery, there is a double symbol. ♀ §

15

CHILDHOOD

Mohammed's father was called Abdullah, meaning slave of Allah. Allah was a high god of the many gods worshipped in the town of Mecca. His father died while his mother was pregnant. He was born circa 570. When he was five years old, his mother died and his grandfather took over his upbringing. Then Mohammed was orphaned for the third time when his grandfather died and his raising was assumed by his uncle, Abu Talib. All were of the Quraysh tribe. These brief facts are the history known about his early childhood.

I115 When Mohammed was eight years old, his grandfather died. He was then taken in by Abu Talib, his uncle. His uncle took him on a trading trip to Syria, which was a very different place from Mecca. Syria was a sophisticated Christian country very much a part of the cosmopolitan culture of the Mediterranean. It was Syrian Christians who gave the Arabs their alphabet. When Mohammed was a child, there had never been a book written in Arabic. Only poems and business correspondence were written in Arabic.

MARRIAGE

♀ I120 When Mohammed was grown, he was hired by the wealthy widow, Khadija, a distant cousin, to act as her agent in trading with Syria. Mohammed had a reputation of good character and good business sense. Trading between Mecca and Syria was risky business because it took skill to manage a caravan and to make the best deal in Syria.

♀
ჼ I120 On one trip Mohammed took one of Khadija's slaves along. When they returned, the slave related a story that a Christian had said Mohammed was destined to be a man of power. On the same trip Mohammed managed to double Khadija's investment. She proposed marriage to him. They married and had six children, two sons who died in childhood, and four daughters who lived to adulthood.

MECCA AS A RELIGIOUS CENTER

In Mecca there was a stone building in the shape of a cube called the Kabah. The Kabah was a religious site that contained many images of several tribal gods. We know of at least six other square stone houses called Kabahs that were in other towns in Arabia. However, Islam holds that the Kabah in Mecca was built by Abraham, the patriarch of the Jews.

The Kabah was the focus of religious rituals and was also a community center. One of Mohammed's ancestors, Qusayy, was a pagan religious leader. Rituals established by Qusayy included prostrations, ritual prayers, and circling the Kabah while praying and drinking from the well called Zam Zam. Other rituals included throwing stones at pillars which symbolized the devil. Most of Islam's rituals come from the aboriginal Arabic religions.

Stones played an important part in the religions of Arabia. The Kabah was made of stone and had an important stone, the Black Stone, built into one corner. It was probably a meteorite and was a composite of several stones. It is small in size, roughly seven inches in diameter. This stone was touched only with the right hand and kissed by pilgrims. All of these native rituals were incorporated into Islam.

The god, Allah, seems to have been a male god of the moon and was probably the god of the Quraysh tribe, Mohammed's tribe. Each tribe had its gods. There was not much organization of the gods, unlike those of the Greeks or Romans.

MECCA

BEGINNING TEACHINGS

CHAPTER 4

These are the limits set up by Allah. Those who obey Allah and His Messenger will be led into the Gardens watered by flowing rivers to live forever. This is the ultimate reward! [Koran 4:13]

I150 Mohammed would take month-long retreats to be alone and practice the Quraysh religion. After the retreat he would go and circumambulate (circle and pray) the Kabah.

I152 At the age of forty Mohammed began to have visions and hear voices. His visions were first shown to him as bright as daybreak during his sleep in the month of Ramadan. Mohammed said that the angel, Gabriel, came to him with a brocade with writing on it and commanded him to read. "What shall I read?" The angel pressed him and said, "Read." Mohammed said again, "What shall I read?" The angel pressed him again tightly and again commanded, "Read!" Again the reply, "What shall I read?"

The angel said:

Koran   96:1 *Recite: In the name of your Lord, Who created man from clots of blood.*

96:3 *Recite: Your Lord is the most generous, Who taught the use of the pen and taught man what he did not know.*

♀   T1150 Khadija, his wife, sent men looking for him and brought him back to the house. He told her that he was afraid that he had gone insane or become an ecstatic poet and that he hated both things. She sent him to her cousin who was a Christian. The cousin told Mohammed that he was a prophet.

♀   I154 Khadija told Mohammed to let her know the next time that Gabriel arrived. When he told her that Gabriel had come, she had Mohammed sit next to her on her right side. She asked, "Can you see Gabriel?" Mohammed said, "Yes," he said. Then she asked him to sit next to her on her left side and asked if he could see Gabriel and Mohammed said that he could. Then she told Mohammed to sit in her lap and asked if Gabriel was still there. Yes. Then she took off her clothes and asked if Gabriel was still there. Mohammed said, "No." Khadija said, "Rejoice, he is an angel, not a devil."

THE FIRST CONVERT

I156 Mohammed's wife was the first convert. From the beginning, she ♀ had encouraged and believed him. She knew that he was of good character and did not think him to be deceived or crazy.

Soon he stopped hearing voices or seeing visions, became depressed and felt abandoned. Then his visions started again.

PRAYER

I157 Mohammed began to pray with a new understanding. At first he performed two prostrations with each prayer. Later he understood that he should use four prostrations per prayer and use two prostrations when he was traveling.

I158 Then, when he was on a mountain, he saw a vision in which Gabriel showed him how to use ritual ablutions as a purification before prayer. He went home and showed his wife, Khadija, that he now understood how the prayer rituals were done and she copied him.

T1162 Mohammed, his wife and nephew, Ali, started praying at the Kabah ♀ incorporating these new rituals of ablutions and prayer with prostrations. A visitor asked about this new ritual and was told that it was a new religion with Mohammed as its prophet.

EARLY ISLAM

The idea of having an Arabian prophet was new. The sources of the native religions were unknown, but the new religion of Islam had a self-declared prophet. The Jews had prophets, and now the Arabs had their own prophet in Mohammed. The religion was called Islam, meaning submission. Those who joined Islam were called Muslims, meaning those who submitted.

I161 A new element was added to the religion. Any person who rejected the revelations of Mohammed would be eternally punished. Only Islam was acceptable.

I166 The Muslims went to the edge of Mecca to pray in order to be alone. One day a group of the Quraysh came upon them and began to mock them and a fight started. Saed, a Muslim, picked up the jaw bone of a camel and struck one of the Quraysh with it and bloodied him. This violence was the first blood to be shed in Islam.

I167 When Mohammed first spoke about his new religion, it did not cause any concern among the Meccans. Then Mohammed began to condemn the ancient religions.

I168 Some of the Quraysh went to Abu Talib, Mohammed's uncle and a respected tribal protector, and said to him, "Your nephew has cursed our gods, insulted our religion, mocked our way of life, criticized our civilization, attacked our virtues, and said that our forefathers were ignorant and in error. You must stop him, or you must let us stop him. We will rid you of him." Abu Talib gave them a soft reply and sent them away.

I169 The Quraysh realized that Abu Talib was not going to help. Mohammed continued to preach Islam and attack them and their lives. Mecca was a small town, everyone knew everyone else. Islam had split the town of Mecca and divided the ruling and priestly tribe.

I170 Things worsened. Soon there was open hostility in Mecca. Quarrels increased, arguments became very heated. Complete disharmony dominated the town. The Quraysh tribe started to abuse the recently converted Muslims, but Mohammed's uncle, Abu Talib, was a respected elder and was able to protect the new Muslims from real harm.

The Koran gives such precise details and direct quotes of their arguments that if you were a Meccan of that day, you would easily recognize the person.

Koran 111:1 *Let the hands of Abu Lahab [Mohammed's uncle and an opponent] die and let him die! His wealth and attainments will not help him. He will be burned in Hell, and his wife will carry the firewood, with a palm fiber rope around her neck.*

I178 Fortunately for Mohammed, the Arabs of Medina were attracted to Islam's message. Since half of their town consisted of Jews, the Arabs of Medina were used to the concept of only one god.

This is the Sunna of Mohammed

PUBLIC TEACHING

CHAPTER 5

Say: Obey Allah and His messenger, but if they reject it, then truly,
Allah does not love those who reject the faith. [Koran 3:32]

At first Mohammed only told close friends and relatives about his message. Then he began to preach more publicly. The Koran condemns those who argue with Mohammed, since to argue against Islam is to be an enemy of Allah. The Koran gives an exact accounting of the arguments of the opponents of Mohammed.

The Koran was not delivered whole, in one piece, but was dribbled out over the years. The Meccans reasoned that if the all-knowing god of the universe, Allah, was the author of the Koran, then why did he not deliver the entire Koran at once, instead of delivering it a piece at a time over the years.

Mohammed continued to preach about Judgment Day, Paradise and Hell:

Koran   43:68 *My servants, there is no fear for you that day, nor will you grieve, because you have believed in Our signs and surrendered your will to Allah. You and your wives shall enter the Garden rejoicing. Trays and goblets of gold will be passed around to them, and they will have everything they desire. They will dwell there forever. This is the Garden that will be given you because of your good deeds in life. There is an abundance of fruit there for you to enjoy.*

43:74 *The guilty, however, will dwell forever in the torment of Hell. The punishment will not be lightened for them, and they will be overwhelmed with despair. We were not unjust toward them. It was they who were unjust. They will cry, "Malik [an angel who is a keeper of Hell], let your Lord put us out of our misery." He will respond, "No! You will remain here." Surely, We have brought the truth to you, but most of you hate the truth.*
43:79 *Do they make plots against you? We also make plots. Do they think that We do not hear their secrets and their private conversations? We do, and Our messengers are there to record them.*

I183 Mohammed continued to preach the glory of Allah and condemn the Quraysh religion. He told them their way of life was wrong and their ancestors would burn in Hell. He cursed their gods, disparaged their religion and divided the community, setting one tribesman against another. The Quraysh felt that this was unbearable. Tolerance had always been their way.

There were many clans, many gods, many religions. Another religion was fine, why did Mohammed demean the other religions?

MORE ARGUMENTS WITH THE MECCANS

I188, 189 Another group of Meccans sent for Mohammed to see if they could settle this painful division of the tribes. They went over old ground, and again Mohammed refused the money and power that was offered. He said they needed to decide whether or not they wanted to suffer in the next world and he had the only solution. If they rejected him and his message, Allah would tend to them. One of the Quraysh said, "Well, if you speak for and represent the only true god, then perhaps his Allah could do something for them."

"This land is dry. Let his Allah send them a river next to Mecca."

"They were cramped being next to the mountains. Let his Allah open up some space by moving the mountains back."

"Our best members are dead. Let your Allah renew them to life and in particular send back the best leader of our tribe, Qusayy. We will ask Qusayy whether or not you speak truly."

I189 Mohammed said that he was sent as a messenger, not to do such work. They could either accept his message or reject it and be subject to the loss. Then one of them said, "If you won't use your Allah to help us, then let your Allah help you. Send an angel to confirm you and prove to us that we are wrong. As long as the angel is present, let him make you a garden and fine home and present you with all the gold and silver you need. If you do this, we will know that you represent Allah and we are wrong." The Quraysh wanted miracles as a proof.

I189 Mohammed did not perform miracles, because such things were not what Allah had appointed him to do.

I189 Then one of the Quraysh said, "Then let the heavens be dropped on us in pieces as you say your Lord could do. If you do not we will not believe." Mohammed said that Allah could do that if Allah wished or he might not if he wished.

I189 They then said, "Did not your Lord know that we would ask you these questions? Then your Lord could have prepared you with better answers. And your Lord could have told you what to tell us if we don't believe. We hear that you are getting this Koran from a man named Al Rahman from another town. We don't believe in Al Rahman. Our conscience is clear. We must either destroy you or you must destroy us. Bring your angels and we will believe them."

1191 Mohammed would go to the Kabah and tell the Meccans what terrible punishments Allah had delivered to others in history who had not believed their prophets. This was now one of his constant themes. Allah destroyed others like them who did not listen to men like Mohammed.

1206 Some of the first Muslims were slaves and the Meccans prosecuted them when they could. Abu Bakr was one of the early converts to Islam. He would later be Mohammed's father-in-law and the first caliph. He was a wealthy man and bought and freed six Muslim slaves to stop their persecution by the Meccans.

This is the Sunna of Mohammed

THE BATTLE THAT CHANGED THE WORLD

CHAPTER 6

*So obey Allah and His messenger. But if you turn your backs
to them, Our messenger is not to blame, for his duty is only to
deliver Our warning clearly. Allah! There is no god but Him!
Let the faithful put their trust in Allah.* [Koran 64:12]

Mohammed was one of the last to leave Mecca for Medina. In Medina
Mohammed built the first mosque. There were now two types of Muslims
in Medina. The native Medinan Muslims were called the Helpers, and the
new arrivals were called the Immigrants.

♀   I335 Ali, Mohammed's cousin, left for Medina three days after Mohammed. Ali spent two nights in a town on the way to Medina. He noticed that
every night a man came to the door of an unmarried Muslim woman. Ali
questioned her about this. She told Ali that the man was bringing stolen
Kafir ritual objects to her and that she would burn them.

THE COVENANT

One reason for Mohammed going to Medina was to arbitrate in a fight
between two Arab tribes, each one had Jewish allies.

One of Mohammed's first actions was to draw up a political charter with
all parties that included the basis of war. The Jews were included in the
charter as allies of the Muslims. All disputes were to be resolved with Mohammed in the role of judge.

MARRIAGE

♀   M177 About seven months after arriving in Medina, Mohammed, aged
fifty-three, consummated his marriage with Aisha, now age nine. She
moved out of her father's house into what was to become a compound of
apartments adjoining the mosque. She was allowed to bring her dolls into
the harem due to her age.

THE JEWS

In Mecca, Mohammed had divided the community into Muslims and
those practicing the native Arabic religions. In Mecca he adopted all the
classical Jewish stories to prove his prophecies and spoke well of the

Jews. However, there were almost no Jews living in Mecca, and therefore, no one to differ with him.

In Medina, half of the population were Jews who let Mohammed know they disagreed with him. So in Medina, Mohammed argued with Jews as well as the Kafir Arabs. Even though there were very few in the town who were Christian, Mohammed argued against them as well. All Kafirs were verbally attacked in Medina.

1415 Thirteen years after he started preaching and one year after going to Medina, Mohammed began to prepare for war as commanded by Allah. He would fight his enemies: the Kafirs.

THE FIRST RAIDS

The idea of raiding Meccan caravans solved two problems for Mohammed. The first was the money would cure the Muslim poverty. Secondly, Mohammed would get his revenge for being driven out of Mecca. The idea of jihad was born at this time.

1416-423 Mohammed sent his fighters out on seven armed raids to find a trade caravan headed to Mecca.

On the eighth try the jihadists found the caravan. They killed one man and captured the rest. The booty and captives were taken back to Medina. There was a small problem. They had raided and killed someone in a sacred month of peace. This violated Arabic tribal custom.

But the Koran said that killing the Kafirs in the sacred months was a moral act. For the Meccans to resist Islam was an offence against Allah, so the killing was justified.

FIGHTING IN ALLAH'S CAUSE—BADR

The next Meccan caravan was large. When the Meccans got wind that the Muslims were going to attack, they sent out a small army to protect it. Mohammed sent out his men to either attack the caravan or do battle with the protecting army.

1433 Mohammed and his men headed out of Medina for what would prove to be one of the most important battles in all of history, a battle that would change the world forever.

1435 Mohammed was cheered. He said, "I see the enemy dead on the ground." They headed towards Badr and camped near there for the night. He sent several scouts to the well at Badr and the scouts found two slaves with water camels. They felt sure they were from the caravan and brought them back to Mohammed. Two of Mohammed's men questioned them as

25

Mohammed was nearby praying. Mohammed wanted to know which group they were facing—the Quraysh caravan or the army under Abu Sufyan. The men replied that they were from the Quraysh. While Mohammed prayed, his men began to beat and torture the captured slaves.

§   1436 Mohammed told his men that the slaves told them the truth until they started to beat and torture them. Then the slaves had lied, but it had been the lie that the Muslims wanted to hear. Mohammed asked the slaves how many of the Meccan army there were and who were the leaders? When they told him, he was delighted and told his warriors that Mecca had sent their best men to be slaughtered.

1440-444 The Meccans marched forth at daybreak. The battle began.

1445 Some arrows flew and one Muslim was killed. Mohammed addressed his army. "By Allah, every man who is slain this day by fighting with courage and advancing, not retreating, will enter Paradise." One of his men had been eating dates said, "You mean that there is nothing between me and Paradise except being killed by the Quraysh?" He flung the dates to the side, picked up his sword and set out to fight. He got his wish and was killed later.

1452 The battle went well for the outnumbered Muslims. After the battle a jihadist brought Mohammed the head of his enemy, Abu Jahl. He said, "Here is the head of the enemy of Allah" and threw it at Mohammed's feet. The Prophet said, "Praise be to Allah."

1455 As the bodies were dragged to a well, one of the Muslims saw the body of his father thrown in. He said, "My father was a virtuous, wise, kind, and cultured man. I had hoped he would become a Muslim. He died a Kafir. His abode is hellfire forever."

Before Islam, the killing of kin and tribal brothers had been forbidden since the dawn of time. After Islam, brother would kill brother and sons would kill their fathers, fighting in Allah's cause—jihad.

1454 The bodies of the Quraysh were thrown into a well. The Apostle of Allah leaned over the well and shouted at the bodies, "Oh people of the well, have you found what Allah promised to be true?" The Muslims were puzzled by his question. Mohammed explained that the dead could hear him.

1459 They set off for Medina with the spoils of war and the prisoners to be ransomed, except for one who had spoken against Mohammed. He was brought in front of the Prophet to be killed, but before the sword struck, he asked, "Who will care for my family?"

M230 The Prophet replied, "Hell!" After he fell dead, Mohammed said, "Unbeliever in Allah and his Prophet and his Book! I give thanks to Allah Who has killed you and made my eyes satisfied."

I481 After war and victory there were the spoils of war to divide. One fifth went to the Apostle, Allah's prophet.

THE AFFAIR OF MOHAMMED'S DAUGHTER

I465 Among the prisoners was Mohammed's son-in-law, Abul-As, who ♀ was also the nephew of Khadija, Mohammed's wife. As a matter of fact, Khadija had asked Mohammed to look for a wife for her nephew, and it had been Mohammed who suggested marriage to their daughter, Zaynab. This was before Mohammed became a prophet and he never opposed Khadija at that time. When Mohammed went to Medina, the Meccans had tried to get Abul-As to divorce Mohammed's daughter, but he refused, even though Abul-As had never become a Muslim himself. Mohammed was fond of him.

I465 But there was a second Meccan, Utba, who had married Mohammed's ♀ second daughter. When the Meccans approached him to divorce Mohammed's daughter, Utba agreed on the condition he could have his pick of two women. They agreed and Utba divorced Mohammed's daughter.

I466 Abul-As was captured at Badr. His wife sent the money for his ran- ♀ som and included with it a necklace that Khadija, Mohammed's wife, had given her on her wedding day. When Mohammed saw the necklace, he softened and asked the captors to forgo the ransom and return Abul-As to his daughter. The captors agreed.

I467 Mohammed set a condition that his daughter, Zaynab, be allowed to ♀ come and see him. So when Abul-As returned to Mecca, he told Zaynab to go to Medina to see Mohammed. She prepared and left on a camel with her brother-in-law. The Meccans decided to chase after them and caught her on the road. One of the Meccans approached with his spear and threatened her. The story is vague, but she may have been pregnant and the panic caused her to abort. Her brother-in-law drew his bow and threatened to kill all of the Meccans.

· I467 The leader of the Meccans, Abu Sufyan, asked him to unstring his ♀ bow and talk. He said, "Look, we have just been humiliated by Mohammed, and now you are taking his daughter to him very publicly. Come back to Mecca and wait until the anger has died down and then leave quietly." And that is what they did. Later he took her away in the middle of the night.

I469 Later when Mohammed sent out raiders, he told them that if they ♀ found one of the two men who threatened his daughter, they were to burn them to death. Later, he told them not to burn them, because only Allah should punish with fire. They should just kill them, instead.

♀ 1470 Zaynab continued to live in Medina, while Abul-As lived in Mecca. Abul-As headed a trading expedition to Syria. Mohammed warriors attacked the caravan and captured all of the goods, while Abul-As escaped to Medina where he hid out with Zaynab. Mohammed agreed that he was not to be harmed, but that he and Zaynab could not have sex since she was a Muslim.

♀ 1470 Mohammed then went to the warriors who had taken Abul-As's property and asked them to return it and they did. Abul-As then submitted to Islam. He and Zaynab were then considered to be married again.

THE RAID ON THE TRIBE OF B. SULAYM

I540-543, T1365 Seven days after Mohammed returned from Badr, there were four more armed raids, but no contact with the enemy, the Kafirs.

Mohammed had become a political force unlike any ever seen before in history. The fusion of religion and politics with a universal mandate created a permanent historic force. Muslims believe there will be no peace until all the world is Islamic. The spoils of war will provide the wealth of Islam. The awe of Mohammed is the fear of Allah.

B1,7,331 *The Prophet said, "I have been given five things which were not given to anyone else before me.*

1. Allah made me victorious by awe, by His frightening my enemies for a distance of one month's journey.

2. The earth has been made for me and for my followers a place for praying and to perform my rituals, therefore anyone of my followers can pray wherever the time of a prayer is due.

3. The spoils of war has been made Halal (lawful) for me yet it was not lawful for anyone else before me.

[...]

Mohammed left Mecca as a preacher and prophet. He entered Medina with about 150 Muslim converts. After a year in Medina, there were about 250-300 Muslims, and most of them were very poor. After the battle of Badr, a new Islam emerged. Mohammed rode out of Medina as a politician and general. Islam became an armed political force with a religious motivation, jihad. All of Arabia would submit to Islam in the coming decade.

This is the Sunna of Mohammed

STRUGGLES

CHAPTER 7

Believers! Be obedient to Allah and His messenger, and do not
turn your backs now that you know the truth. Do not be like
the ones who say, "We hear," but do not obey. [Koran 8:20]

1226 Umar was a physically strong man who was influential in Mecca. ♀
His sister and husband submitted to Islam (became Muslims) but Umar,
at this time, hated it. He strapped on his sword and went out looking for
Mohammed. One of his friends saw him and told him that he should deal
with his own family first. Did Umar not know that his sister and her husband
had submitted to Islam? He went to their house, and when he got there,
he could hear a verse from the Koran being recited. Umar stormed in and
demanded to know more about the "garbage" he had just heard. He accused
his sister of being a Muslim and hit her. When she cried, his heart softened.
Umar read the Koran verses and became convinced that Mohammed was
right and he went to Mohammed and submitted to Islam.

1231 With Umar's conversion, Islam became stronger and the Meccans ♀
decided to try a boycott as a non-violent way to pressure Mohammed. So
the Quraysh posted a notice in the Kabah that no Meccan should marry any
Muslim woman or sell them food.

1239 Some Meccans approached Mohammed and said, "Let us worship
what you worship. Then you worship what we worship. If what you
worship is better than what we worship, then we will take a share of your
worship. And if what we worship is better, then you can take a share of
that." This caused Mohammed to compromise his message.

THE SATANIC VERSES

T1192 Mohammed was always thinking of ways to persuade all the
Meccans to accept Islam. It came to him that the three gods of the Quraysh
could intercede with Allah. Mohammed said, "These are the exalted high
flying cranes whose intercession is approved." The Meccans were delighted
and happy. When Mohammed led prayers at the Kabah, all the Meccans,
Muslims and Kafirs, took part. The Quraysh hung about after the combined
service and remarked how happy they were. The tribe had been unified in
worship, as before Islam.

Then Mohammed said that he had been deceived by Satan. There was
no bridge between Islam and the religion of the Meccans. The retraction by

Mohammed made the relations between Islam and the Meccans far worse than they had ever been.

THE POET'S SUBMISSION

1252 Al Dausi was a poet of some standing in Arabia. When he visited Mecca, Al Dausi went to the mosque and heard Mohammed preaching. He liked what he heard and followed Mohammed home. They spoke for some time and Al Dausi decided to submit to Islam.

♀ 1253 He then entered his home and told his wife, "Leave me, I want nothing to do with you." She cried, "Why?" Al Dausi said, "Islam has divided us and I now follow Mohammed." She replied, "Then your religion is my religion." He then instructed her in Islam.

The Koran is constant in its admonitions about with whom a Muslim should be friends.

> Koran 4:144 *Believers! Do not take Kafirs as friends over fellow believers. Would you give Allah a clear reason to punish you?*

§ 1260 There was one Christian in Mecca in whom Mohammed took an interest. He was a Christian slave who ran a booth in the market. Mohammed would go and speak with him at length. The Meccans believed that Mohammed was making up the "revelations of Allah". This led to the Quraysh claiming that what Mohammed said in the Koran came from the Christian slave.

THE NIGHT JOURNEY

1264 One night as he lay sleeping, Mohammed said that the angel nudged him with his foot. Mohammed awoke. They went out the door and found a white animal, half mule and half donkey. Its feet had wings and could move to the horizon in one step. Gabriel put Mohammed on the white animal and off they went to Jerusalem to the site of the Temple.

1264 There at the temple were Jesus, Abraham, Moses and other prophets. Mohammed led them in prayer. Gabriel brought Mohammed two bowls. One was filled with wine and the other was filled with milk. Mohammed took the one with milk and drank it. That was the right choice.

♀ 1265 Aisha, Mohammed's favorite wife, used to say that Mohammed never
§ left the bed that night, however, his spirit soared. When Mohammed went out into Mecca to tell the story of his Night Journey, the owner of the home where Mohammed had slept sent her black female slave to follow Mohammed and see how the Meccans reacted to his story.

1266 Mohammed reported that Abraham looked exactly like himself. Moses was a ruddy-faced man, tall, thin, and with curly hair. Jesus was light skinned with reddish complexion and freckles and lank hair.

1269 Then he saw women tortured by hanging from their breasts. These ♀ women had given birth to bastards on their husbands. Mohammed said that Allah hates women who birth bastards. They deprive the true sons of their inheritance and learn the secrets of the harem.

1270 Abraham took Mohammed into Paradise, and there was a beautiful ♀ woman with red lips. Mohammed asked who she belonged to, for she was very attractive to him. She belong to Zaid (Mohammed's adopted son). When he got back, Mohammed told Zaid of this.

1272 Mohammed continued to preach Islam and condemn the old Arabic religions. There were those of the Quraysh who defended their culture and religion and argued with him. Mohammed called them mockers and cursed one of them, "Oh Allah, blind him and kill his son."

The Koran records the actual quotes of Mohammed's opponents.

> Koran   41:26 *The Kafirs say, "Do not listen to this Koran. Instead speak during its reading so that you might gain the upper hand." But We will certainly give the Kafirs a taste of a terrible punishment, and We will repay them for their evil deeds. The reward of Allah's enemies is the Fire. The Fire will be their immortal home, a fitting reward for rejecting Our signs.*

1272 One day Mohammed stood with the angel, Gabriel, as the Quraysh performed the rituals of their religion. Among them were the leaders who defended their native culture and religion and opposed Mohammed. When the first leader passed by Gabriel, Gabriel threw a leaf in his face and blinded him. Gabriel then caused the second one to get dropsy which killed him. Gabriel caused the third man to develop an infection which killed him. The fourth man was caused later to step on a thorn which killed him. Gabriel killed the last man who dared to not worship Allah with a brain disease.

MOHAMMED'S PROTECTOR AND WIFE BOTH DIE

1278 Mohammed's protector was his uncle, Abu Talib. When Abu Talib fell ill, some of the leaders of the Quraysh came to his bedside. They said to him, "Please work out a compromise between Mohammed and us."

1278 So Abu Talib called Mohammed to his side. "Nephew, these men have come so that you can give them something and they can give you something." Mohammed said, "If they will give me one word, they can rule the Persians and the Arabs. And they must accept Allah as their Lord and renounce their gods."

1278 Mohammed turned his attention to his dying uncle. He asked him to become a Muslim and then Mohammed could intercede for him on judgment day. His uncle died as a Kafir.

Abu Talib had taken the orphan Mohammed into his home and raised him. He took Mohammed on caravan trading missions to Syria and taught him how to be a businessman. Abu Talib was the clan chief who protected Mohammed's life when the rest of Mecca wanted to harm him. Abu Talib was Mohammed's life and security, but he was damned to Hell.

After Abu Talib's death, the pressure on Mohammed was greater. It reached the point where one of the Quraysh threw dust at Mohammed. This was the worst persecution that happened in Mecca.

♀ The death of his wife, Khadija, had no political effect, but it was a blow to Mohammed. His wife was his chief confidant, and she consoled him.

MARRIAGE

♀ WM113 About three months after the death of Khadija, Mohammed married Sauda, a widow and a Muslim.

♀ WM113 Abu Bakr, an early wealthy Muslim, had a daughter, Aisha, who was six years old. Soon after marrying Sauda, Mohammed was betrothed to Aisha, who was to become his favorite wife. The consummation of the marriage would not take place until she turned nine.

> M031,5977 *Aisha reported Mohammed having said: I saw you in a dream*
> *for three nights when an angel brought you to me in a silk cloth and he*
> *said: Here is your wife, and when I removed (the cloth) from your face,*
> *lo, it was yourself, so I said: If this is from Allah, let Him carry it out.*

1279 With Abu Talib's death, Mohammed needed political allies. Mohammed went to the city of Taif, about fifty miles away, with one servant. In Taif he met with three brothers who were politically powerful. Mohammed called them to Islam and asked them to help him in his struggles with those who would defend their native religions.

His trip was a failure and he returned to Mecca.

THE BEGINNING OF POWER AND JIHAD IN MEDINA

Medina was about a ten-day journey from Mecca, but since ancient times the Medinans had come to Mecca for the fairs. Medina was half Jewish and half Arabian, and there was an ongoing tension between the two. The Jews worked as farmers and craftsmen and were literate. They were the wealthy class, but their power was slowly waning. In times past, the Arabs had raided and stolen from the Jews, who retaliated by saying that one day a prophet would come and lead them to victory over the Arabs. In spite of the tensions, the Arab tribe of Khazraj were allied with them.

1294 At the next fair in Mecca, many of the new Muslims from Medina showed up. During the early part of the night, about seventy of them left the caravan to meet with Mohammed. He recited the Koran and said, "I invite your allegiance on the basis that you protect me as you would your children." The Medinans gave their oath. After the oath, one of them asked about their now-severed ties to the Jews of Medina. If they helped Mohammed with arms and they were successful, would he go back to Mecca? Mohammed smiled and said, "No, blood is blood, and blood not to be paid for is blood not to be paid for." Blood revenge and its obligation were common to them. "I will war against them who war against you and be at peace with those at peace with you."

1312 One of the two women who gave their oath of allegiance was named Nusayba. She took part in the battle of Yamama and was wounded twelve times.

1299 One of the Medinans said to those who made the pledge, "Do you realize to what you are committing yourselves in pledging your support to this man? It is war against all. If you think that if you lose your property and your best are killed, and then you would give him up, then quit now. But if you think that you will be loyal to your oath if you lose your property and your best are killed, then take him, for it will profit you now and in Paradise." They asked what they would receive for their oath, Mohammed promised them Paradise. They all shook hands on the deal.

BACK IN MEDINA

1304 Back in Medina, the Muslims now practiced their new religion openly. But most of the Arabs still practiced their ancient tribal religions. The Muslims would desecrate the old shrines and ritual objects. They would even break into houses and steal ritual objects and throw them into the latrines. On one occasion, they killed a dog and tied the dog's body to a ritual object and thew it into the latrine.

MIGRATION

Mohammed had been driven out of Mecca and now migrated to Medina for refuge and a new home.

I314 The Muslim Medinans had pledged to support Mohammed in war and to help the Muslims from Mecca. The Muslims in Mecca left and went to Medina. The Muslims from both Mecca and Medina were about to be tested.

This is the Sunna of Mohammed

MEDINA

THE JEWS

CHAPTER 8

Do they not know that whoever opposes Allah and His
Messenger will abide in the Fire of Hell, where they will
remain forever? This is the great shame. [Koran 9:63]

When Mohammed arrived in Medina about half the town were Jews. There were three tribes of Jews and two tribes of Arabs. Almost none of the Jews had Hebrew names. They were Arabs to some degree. At the same time many of the Arabs' religious practices contained elements of Judaism. The Jews were farmers and tradesmen and lived in their own fortified quarters. In general, they were better educated and more prosperous than the Arabs.

Before Mohammed arrived, there had been bad blood and killing among the tribes. The last battle had been fought between the two Arab tribes, but each of the Jewish tribes had joined the battle with their particular Arab allies. In addition to that tension between the two Arab tribes, there was a tension between the Jews and the Arabs. The division of the Jews and fighting on different sides was condemned by Mohammed. The Torah preached that the Jews should be unified, and they failed in this.

All of these quarrelsome tribal relationships were one reason that Mohammed was invited to Medina, but the result was further polarization, not unity. The new split was between Islam and those Arabs and their Jewish partners who resisted Islam.

1351 About this time, the leaders of the Jews spoke out against Mohammed. The rabbis began to ask him difficult questions. Doubts and questions arose about his doctrine. But for Mohammed, doubts about Allah were evil. However, two of the Jewish Arabs joined with Mohammed as Muslims. They believed him when he said that he was the Jewish prophet that came to fulfill the Torah.

THE REAL TORAH IS IN THE KORAN

Mohammed said repeatedly that the Jews and Christians corrupted their sacred texts in order to conceal the fact that he was prophesied in their scriptures. The stories in the Koran are similar to those of the Jew's scriptures, but they make different points. In the Koran, all of the stories found in Jewish scripture indicated that Allah destroyed those cultures that did not listen to their messengers. According to Mohammed, the scriptures of the Jews had been changed to hide the fact that Islam is the true religion and that he was the last prophet of the Jews.

1369 The Jews' sins are so great that Allah has changed them into apes. Still they will not learn and refuse to admit that Mohammed is their prophet. They know full well the truth and hide and confuse others. Even when they say to Mohammed they believe, they conceal their resistance.

> Koran 2:63 *And remember, Children of Israel, when We made a covenant with you and raised Mount Sinai before you saying, "Hold tightly to what We have revealed to you and keep it in mind so that you may guard against evil." But then you turned away, and if it had not been for Allah's grace and mercy, you surely would have been among the lost. And you know those among you who sinned on the Sabbath. We said to them, "You will be transformed into despised apes." So we used them as a warning to their people and to the following generations, as well as a lesson for the Allah-fearing.*

1370 The Jews have understood the truth of Mohammed and then changed their scriptures to avoid admitting that Mohammed is right.

MOHAMMED TRULY FOLLOWS THE RELIGION OF ABRAHAM

♀ 1375 A group of rabbis came to Mohammed and asked him, "Why does a boy resemble his mother if the sperm comes from the father?" Mohammed replied that a man's fluid is thick and white and a woman's fluid is yellow and thin. The child resembles the mother or the father depending upon whose fluid was on top.

♀ 1394 The Jews asked Mohammed to deliver judgment against a married man and a married woman who had committed adultery. Mohammed delivered the full judgment found in the Torah, which was stoning. The Jews had stopped using capital punishment. So the couple was brought to the mosque and they were stoned to death. When the man felt the first stone, he crouched over the woman until they were both dead.

> [B3,41,596;B4,51,9;B7,63,216;B9,83,15;B9,83,16;B9,83,18;B9,83,23;]
> *During the lifetime of Mohammed, a Jew attacked a girl and took some silver ornaments she was wearing and crushed her head between two stones. Her relatives brought her to Mohammed while she was taking her last breaths and was unable to speak. He asked her who had killed her, and mentioned different names. She shook her head with each name,*

until Mohammed finally mentioned the name of the criminal, and she nodded. So the Jew was questioned until he confessed. Then Mohammed ordered that the head of that Jew be crushed between two stones.

AN OMINOUS CHANGE

1381 In Mecca, Mohammed spoke well of the Jews, who were very few. In Medina there were many Jews and his relations with them were tense. Up to now Mohammed had led prayer facing in the direction of Jerusalem. Now the *kiblah*, direction of prayer, was changed to the Kabah in Mecca. Some of the Jews came to him and asked why he had changed the direction of prayer. After all, he said that he followed the religion of Abraham. They could not see that their rejection of his role as a prophet meant that they were enemies and things were going to change.

Since Islam is the successor to Judaism, Allah was the successor to Jehovah. It was actually Allah who had been the deity of the Jews and the Jews had deliberately hidden this fact by corrupting the scriptures. For this, Muslims believe, the Jews have been cursed.

THE AFFAIR OF THE JEWS OF QAYNUQA

1545 There were three tribes of Jews in Medina, one of these was the Beni Qaynuqa, who were goldsmiths and lived in a stronghold in their quarters. It is said by Mohammed that they broke the treaty that had been signed when Mohammed came to Medina. How they did this is unclear.

1545 Mohammed assembled the Jews in their market and said: "Oh Jews, be careful that Allah does not bring vengeance upon you like what happened to the Quraysh. Become Muslims. You know that I am the prophet that was sent you. You will find that in your scriptures."

1545 They replied: "Oh, Mohammed, you seem to think that we are your people. Don't fool yourself. You may have killed and beaten a few merchants of the Quraysh, but we are men of war and real men."

1546 Some time later Mohammed besieged the Beni Qaynuqa Jews in their quarters. Neither of the other two Jewish tribes came to their support. Finally the Jews surrendered, expecting to be slaughtered after their capture.

But one of the Jews' old allies persuaded Mohammed not to kill them. Mohammed exiled the Jews and took all of their wealth and goods.

THE RAID TO AL QARADA

1547 Mohammed's victory at Badr and ongoing jihad caused the Quraysh to choose a different route to Syria. They hired a new guide to take them over the new route. Mohammed had received intelligence about their route and sent a party to raid them. They were carrying a great deal of silver when the caravan stopped at a watering hole. The Muslims surprised them and the Quraysh managed to escape but Mohammed's men were able to steal all the caravan's goods, including the silver. The stolen goods were delivered to Mohammed in Medina.

THE ASSASSINATION OF AL ASHRAF, THE JEW

1548 When Al Ashraf, a Jew of Medina, heard that two of his friends had been killed at Badr, he said that it was better to be in the grave than on earth with Mohammed. So the "enemy of Allah" composed some poems bewailing the loss of his friends and attacking Islam.

♀ T1369 Then Al Ashraf wrote a sexual poem about a Muslim woman.

1551 When Mohammed heard of Al Ashraf's critical poetry about his politics, he said, "Who will rid me of Al Ashraf?" A Muslim said, "I will kill him for you." Days later, Mohammed found out that his assassin was not doing anything, including eating or drinking. Mohammed summoned him and asked what was going on. The man replied that he had taken on a task that was too difficult for him to do. Mohammed said that it was a duty which he should try to do. The assassin said, "Oh Apostle of Allah, I will have to tell a lie." The Prophet said, "Say what you like, you are free in the matter."

1552 Through the use of lies three Muslims were able to kill Al Ashraf. When they returned to Mohammed, he was praying. They told him that they had killed the enemy of Allah. Their attack terrorized all the Jews. There was no Jew in Medina who was not afraid.

KILL ANY JEW THAT FALLS INTO YOUR POWER

1554 The Apostle of Allah said, "Kill any Jew who falls into your power." Hearing this Muhayyisa fell upon a Jewish merchant who was a business associate and killed him. Muhayyisa's brother was not a Muslim and asked him how he could kill a man who had been his friend and partner in many business deals. The Muslim said that if Mohammed had asked him to kill his brother he would have done it immediately. His brother said, "You mean that if Mohammed said to cut off my head you would do it?" "Yes," was the reply. The older brother then said, "By Allah, any religion which brings you to this is marvelous." And he decided then and there to become a Muslim.

This is the Sunna of Mohammed

JIHAD, A SETBACK

CHAPTER 10

But those who disobey Allah and His Messenger and go
beyond His limits, will be led into the Fire to live forever,
and it will be a humiliating torment! [Koran 4:14]

THE BATTLE OF UHUD

The Meccans had lost at the battle of Badr, but they raised an army and returned to fight the Muslims at Uhud, near Medina.

1560 When they saw the Meccans, Mohammed said, "Let there be no fighting until I give the word." Mohammed placed 50 archers to protect his rear and flank. They must not move but hold that ground.

♀ 1562 The morrow came and the battle was to begin. Now the Meccans had brought their women for the sole purpose urging on the men. Men do not want to be cowards in front of women. The women began to beat their tambourines and chant poetry:

> *If you advance we will hug you*
> *And place soft rugs beneath you*
> *If you retreat we will leave you*
> *Leave and no more love you.*

♀
⚥ 1557 Hind, a Meccan woman, had a black slave called Washi, who was an expert with the javelin. She told Washi that if he could kill Hamza, Islam's greatest fighter, [Hamza had killed Hind's uncle at Badr] he would give him his freedom. On the way to the battle, whenever Hind saw Washi, she would say, "Come on, you father of blackness, satisfy your vengeance and ours."

⚥ 1557 During the battle Washi hung near the edge of the fighting and looked for Hamza. Hamza fought like a lion as Washi watched. As Hamza fought one of the Meccans, he said, "Come here, you son of a clitoris cutter." Hamza then killed the man whose mother performed the female circumcision [removed the girl's clitoris, common surgery in Arabia.] Then Washi threw his javelin and killed Hamza. Washi was now free and left the field.

The Muslims lost because the archers did not hold their position, as instructed, and instead they ran to the Meccan camp to steal their goods.

The Meccans won, but they did not press their advantage and let Mohammed escape.

1578 Hind and other women went through the battlefield and mutilated ♀ the corpses. Hind cut off their ears and noses to make them into bracelets. Hind removed Hamza's liver and chewed it raw.

> We have rewarded you for Badr
> Continued war is violent
> I was broken by the loss of my father and brother
> I have fulfilled my vengeance
> Washi has slacked the burning in my breast
> Thank you Washi.   —Hind

1586 The dead Muslims were buried in the battlefield. Mohammed said, ♀ "I testify that all who are wounded in jihad [fighting in Allah's cause] will be raised by Allah with his bleeding wounds smelling like the finest perfume." Mohammed heard the women weeping for their dead, but he wanted wailing for his uncle Hamza as well. So the women wailed for Hamza and Mohammed felt better.

The Muslims had lost because they did not obey Mohammed's orders. So the Koran says that from now on Muslims must obey Mohammed in all things. They were not to lose courage, as there would be opportunity in the future to get more war booty.

1606 The Koran says that the success that the Kafirs experienced was temporary. They would grow in their evil and be punished. Allah would not leave the believers in this state. But this trial would separate the weak from the strong. Those who have wealth should spend it on jihad.

ASSASSINATION AS JIHAD

M276 After Uhud, several Kafir tribes allied themselves under the leadership of the Meccan, Sufyan Ibn Khalid. Mohammed dispatched an assassin to kill him, for without his leadership the coalition would fall apart. So an assassin, named Abdullah, joined Sufyan's forces and waited until he was alone with him. Once he was alone with him, he killed Sufyan and cut off his head and went back to Medina.

M276 Abdullah then went straight to Mohammed. Mohammed welcomed him and asked him how it went. Abdullah presented Mohammed with the head of his enemy. Mohammed was gratified and presented him with his walking stick. He said, "This is a token between you and me on the day of resurrection. Very few will have such to lean on in that day." Abdullah attached it to his sword scabbard. This incident is one of many that make beheadings Sunna.

THE RAID ON THE MUSTALIQ TRIBE

♀ 1725 When Mohammed heard that the Arab tribe, the Mustaliq, were opposed to him and were gathering against him, he set out with his army to attack. He found them at a watering hole and combat started. Islam was victorious and the Mustaliq and their women, children, and goods were taken as spoils of war and distributed to the fighters.

♀ 1729 The captives of the tribe of Mustaliq were parceled out as spoils. There was a ransom price set upon their heads. If the ransom were not paid then the people were treated as spoils and slaves. Now, one such slave was a beautiful woman with a high price on her. She came to Mohammed and asked him to see if the price could be reduced. Mohammed had a better idea. He paid the ransom and the beautiful woman became wife number seven.

1729 This marriage had a side effect. The captives were tribal relatives and were related to Mohammed's new wife. They were all released without ransom.

THE DEATH OF A POETESS

♀ 1996 There was a poetess who wrote a poem against Islam. Mohammed said, "Who will rid me of Marwan's daughter?" One of his followers, a blind man, heard him and on that very night he went to the woman's home to kill her.

♀ M239 The blind assassin was able to do the work in the dark as the woman slept. Her other children lay in the room, but her babe lay on her breast. The stealthy assassin removed the child and drove the knife into her with such force that he pinned her to the bed.

1996 In the morning he went to Mohammed and told him. Mohammed said, "You have helped Allah and his Apostle."

M239 Mohammed turned to the people in the mosque, he said, "If you wish to see a man who has assisted Allah and his Prophet, look here." Omar cried, "What, the blind Omeir!" "No," said Mohammed, "call him Omeir the Seeing."

♀ 1996 The poetess had five sons and the assassin went to them and taunted them saying, "I killed Bint Marwan, Oh sons. Withstand me if you can; don't keep me waiting." Islam became powerful that day and many became Muslims when they saw the power of Islam.

This is the Sunna of Mohammed

THE CHRISTIANS

*It is such as obey Allah and His Apostle, and fear Allah
and do right, that will win.* [Koran 24:52]

1404 While some Christians visited Medina, they argued religion with
Mohammed. They held forth with the doctrine of the Trinity and the divinity of Christ. Mohammed later laid out the Islamic version of the Christian
doctrine. The Koran tells in detail the Islamic story of Jesus, who is just
another of Allah's prophets, and that the Trinity of the Christians is Allah,
Jesus and Mary.

1406 No one has power except through Allah. Allah gave the prophet Jesus the power of raising the dead, healing the sick, making birds of clay and
having them fly away. Allah gave Jesus these signs as a mark of his being a
prophet. But Allah did not give the powers of appointing kings, or the ability to change night to day. This lack of power shows that Jesus was a man,
not part of the Trinity. If he were part of God, then all powers would have
been in his command. Then he would not have to have been under the do-
minion of kings. Islam holds that it knows the true nature of all religions, in
particular Christianity and Judaism.

MARY, THE MOTHER OF JESUS

1407 Imran was the father of Moses, Aaron and Mary, the mother of Jesus.[1]

Koran 19:16 *And mention Mary in the Scripture, when she withdrew from her
family to a place in the East. She took a veil to screen herself from them.
Then We sent Our spirit [Gabriel] to her in the form of a perfect man. She
said, "I seek protection from you with Merciful Allah. If you fear Him, then
do not come near me."*

19:19 *He said, "I am merely your Lord's messenger. I come to announce to
you the gift of a holy son."*
19:20 *She said, "How can I have a son when no man has touched me, and I
am chaste?"*
19:21 *He said, "Even so, it will happen. Your Lord says, 'That is easy for Me.'
We will make him a sign for all men and a mercy from Us. It is something
that is decreed." And she conceived him, and she withdrew with him to a*

---

1   This version of history is at variance with Christian doctrine. Jesus was
born 1,600 years after Moses.

43

remote place. When the pain of childbirth drove her to the trunk of a palm-tree, she said, "If only I had died before this."

19:24 But a voice from below her said, "Do not grieve; your Lord has provided a stream beneath you. Shake the trunk of the palm-tree towards yourself; it will drop fresh ripe dates upon you. So eat and drink and dry your eyes. And if you should see any man, say, 'I have promised a fast to Allah. I will speak to no one today.'"

1407-8 Christ spoke in the cradle and then spoke to men as a grown man. Speaking from the cradle is a sign of his being a prophet. Christ's prophethood was confirmed by making clay birds fly. It was by Allah's power, that Christ healed the blind, the lepers, and raised the dead.

Koran   *19:27 Later, she brought the baby to her people, carrying him in her arms. They said, "Mary, you have come with an amazing thing. Sister of Aaron, your father was not a wicked man, and your mother was not unchaste." But she merely pointed to the baby. They said, "How can we speak with an infant in a cradle?" The child said, "Surely, I am the servant of Allah. He has given me the Book and has made me a prophet. He has made me blessed wherever I am; and has urged me to pray and give alms, as long as I live; and to be dutiful to my mother; and He has not made me arrogant or miserable. The peace of Allah was on me the day I was born, and will be on me the day that I die; and on the day I will be resurrected."*

19:34 This was Jesus, the son of Mary; this is a statement of truth about which they [Christians] dispute. It does not befit the majesty of Allah to father a son. Glory be to Him! When He decrees something, He only needs to say, "Be," and it is. Surely, Allah is my Lord and your Lord, so serve Him. That is the right path.

1408 Christ only comes through Allah. Christ's signs of being a prophet come only from Allah. Jesus enjoins others to worship Allah, not him. But when the people refused to hear him, the Disciples came forth to help him with his mission. The Disciples were servants of Allah and were Muslims just like Christ.

1409 Christ was not crucified, as written in the Bible. When the Jews plotted against Christ, they found Allah to be the best plotter. Allah took Jesus up directly to him and will refute those who say he was crucified and was resurrected. On the final day, the Day of Resurrection, those who follow Christ but do not believe in his divinity will be blessed. Those who insist that Christ is God, part of the Trinity, and reject true faith will be punished in Hell.

This is the Sunna of Mohammed

JIHAD, THE JEWS SUBMIT

CHAPTER 11

Those who oppose Allah and His Messenger will be laid low.
Allah has declared, "Surely I will be victorious, along with My
messengers." Truly Allah is strong and mighty. [Koran 58:20]

CLEANSING

Mohammed attacked the second of the remaining two Jewish tribes in
Medina. The Jews would not admit that he was a real prophet and for this
they would pay. So Mohammed put the Jews under siege and burned their
date palm plantations. The other Jews would not help them. The losing
Jews cut a deal and got to leave alive with all they could carry.

Since there was no actual fighting and the jihadists did no work, Mohammed got all of the booty.

The burning of the date palms violated ancient Arabic tribal customs.
But the Koran approved the burning and said that it was a moral act against
the Kafir Jews.

THE BATTLE OF THE TRENCH

The Meccans came back to Medina to fight against Islam. But Mohammed had spies in Mecca, so he knew they were coming. At the suggestion of
a Muslim who had been to Persia, the Medinan Muslims built a defensive
trench.

1677-683 Mohammed was able to use his agents to sow discord among
those allied against him. The trench defense frustrated the Meccans. The
weather was bad, and the allies were distrustful of each other. In terms
of actual combat only a handful of men were killed over the twenty-day
siege. The Meccans broke camp and went back home. It was a victory for
Mohammed.

1680 While the armies were facing each other, Hassan was back at a fort.
A Jew was seen going around the fort and Hassan was afraid that he would
find a way in. Hassan's wife said that Hassan should go down and kill the
Jew. But Hassan was a poet who wrote satire for Mohammed and he was
not about to take up arms and told his wife so. The wife took a club and
went outside and beat the Jew to death. She went back to the fort and told
Hassan to go and strip the body. [The killing was an act of jihad and the kill-
er got to take the goods as booty.] But Hassan refused to do even that much.

45

THE SOLUTION FOR THE JEWS

1684 That same day the angel Gabriel came to Mohammed at noon. He asked if Mohammed were through fighting. Gabriel and the angels were going to attack the last Jewish tribe in Medina. Gabriel said, "Allah commands you to go to the Jews. I am headed there now to shake their stronghold."

Mohammed put the Jews under siege. They surrendered and submitted to the judgment of Saed, an old ally.

1688 The Jews decided to let a Muslim they thought was their friend, Saed, deliver judgment if they surrendered to Mohammed. Saed's judgment was simple. Kill all the men. Take their property and take the women and children as captives. Mohammed said, "You have given the judgment of Allah."

1690 The captives were taken into Medina. They dug trenches in the market place of Medina. It was a long day, but 600-700 Jews were beheaded that day. Mohammed and his twelve-year-old wife, Aisha, sat and watched the slaughter the entire day and into the night. The Apostle of Allah had every male Jew killed.

> [B5,59,362]
>
> The Bani An-Nadir and Bani Quraiza violated their peace treaty with Mohammed. He exiled the former and treated the latter with lenience, allowing them to remain in their lands in Medina. When the Bani Quraiza fought Mohammed again, he killed their men and distributed their women and children as slaves among the Muslims. Those who came to Mohammed and embraced Islam were granted safety. He exiled all Jews from Medina.

1691 Only one of the female Jews was killed. She sat with Aisha the entire time the males were being beheaded and laughed and talked. Then a voice called the Jew's name and Aisha asked why she was being called. The Jew said that she had done something. She was taken away and beheaded. The details of this killing are vague.

1693 Mohammed took the property, wives and children of the Jews, and divided it up amongst the Muslims. Mohammed took his one-fifth of the slaves and sent a Muslim with the female Jewish slaves to a nearby city where the women were sold for pleasure. Mohammed invested the money from the sale of the female slaves for horses and weapons.

1693 There was one last share of the spoils for Mohammed. The most beautiful Jewess became his slave for pleasure.

1696-7 In the battle of the Trench it was Allah who had won the day. Allah gives the Muslim his strength and will. No matter what the Kafirs do Allah will triumph. Allah totally approves of the killing of the Jews, enslaving the women and children. It was good to give the Jew's property to the Muslim warriors. After all, Allah wanted it done and helped to do it.

Koran 33:25 *And Allah drove back the Kafirs in their wrath, and they gained nothing by it. Allah aided the believers in the war, for Allah is strong and mighty. He brought down some of the People of the Book [the Jews] out of their fortresses to aid the confederates and to strike terror into their hearts. Some you killed, and others you took captive. He made you heirs of their land, their homes, and their possessions, and even gave you another land on which you had never before set foot. Allah has power over everything. [Hundreds of male Jews were executed, their property taken, and women and children enslaved.]*

THE KILLING OF THE JEW, SALLAM

I714-6 A Jew named Sallam helped to plan and organize the confederation of the tribes that attacked Mohammed in the Battle of the Trench. Mohammed sent five Muslim men to assassinate Sallam. When the men had done their work, they returned to Mohammed and fell to arguing as to who actually killed Sallam. Mohammed demanded to see their swords. He examined them one by one and then pointed to the sword that had been the killing weapon, since it still had food on it still from the thrust to the victim's stomach.

This is the Sunna of Mohammed

JIHAD, THE FIRST DHIMMIS

CHAPTER 12

Those who obey the Messenger, obey Allah. As for those who turn away
from you, We have not sent you to watch over them. [Koran 4:80]

TREATY OF AL HUDAYBIYA

Mohammed decided it was time for the Muslims to make a pilgrimage to Mecca and the Kabah. But the Meccans would not let the Muslims enter, even though they were unarmed and in pilgrimage clothing. So Mohammed parlayed with the Meccans.

1747 They drew up a treaty to the effect that there would be no war for ten years, there would be no hostilities, and no one could convert to Islam without their guardians' permission. In turn the Muslims could come next year and stay for three days in Mecca, but they could not enter this year.

1748 Many of the Muslims were depressed. Mohammed had promised that they could enter Mecca. Now they could not. Before they left they sacrificed the camels and shaved their heads, doing as many of the rituals as they could without getting into Mecca.

1749 On the way back to Medina, Mohammed added to the Koran, the sura [Koran chapter] called Victory, about this treaty. The Muslims who held back [the desert Arabs, Bedouins] and did not come on the pilgrimage would not profit by receiving any spoils of war. And there was more war to come in the future.

1750 This was a victory for Islam because the government of Mecca dealt with Mohammed as an independent political power. Because of this power many more Arabs were attracted to Islam.

♀ 1755 The treaty declared that Mohammed was to return the women of Medina who migrated from Mecca. But Mohammed decided to return the dowries of those women who had come from Mecca to become Muslims without permission of their guardians. Normally, he would have kept the women and the dowries. He also asked the Meccans to return the dowries of those Kafir women who had left Medina to live in Mecca.

KHAYBAR

1756 After the treaty of Al Hudaybiya, Mohammed stayed in Medina for about two months before he collected his army and marched to the forts of

Khaybar, a community of wealthy Jewish farmers who lived in a village of separate forts about 100 miles from Medina.

1758 Mohammed seized the forts one at a time. Among the captives was a ♀ beautiful Jewess named Safiya. Mohammed took her for his sexual pleasure. One of his men had first chosen her for his own slave of pleasure, but Mohammed traded him two of her cousins for Safiya. Mohammed always got first choice of the spoils of war and the women.

1759 On the occasion of Khaybar, Mohammed put forth new orders about ♀ sex with captive women. If the woman was pregnant, she was not to be used 🜨 for sex until after the birth of the child. Nor were any women to be used for sex who were unclean with regards to the Muslim laws about menstruation.

1764 Mohammed knew that there was a large treasure hidden somewhere in Khaybar, so he brought forth the Jew who he thought knew the most about it and questioned him. The Jew denied any knowledge. Mohammed told one of his men, "Torture the Jew until you extract what he has." So the Jew was staked on the ground, and a small fire built on his chest to get him to talk. When the man was nearly dead and still would not talk, Mohammed had him released and taken to one of his men whose brother had been killed in the fight. This Muslim got the pleasure of cutting off the tortured Jew's head.

1763 Mohammed had his freed slave, Bilal, to go and get the two best ♀ looking women and bring them to him, since he always got his pick. Bilal brought the women past their dead husbands. One of them began to shriek and pour dust on her head. Mohammed said, "Take this she-devil away from me." Then he threw his mantle over Safiya so that the men would know she was his, either as a sex slave or wife. Mohammed then told Bilal, "Do you not have any compassion, bringing these two women past their dead husbands?"

[B2,14,68;B3,34,431;B3,34,437;B4,52,143;B5,59,512;B5,59,513;B5,59,522;B5,59,523]

After conquering Khaybar, Mohammed was told of the beauty of Safiya, whose husband had been killed. She was a captive, but he freed her as a marriage gift, and so chose her for his bride. He brought her with the army until they reached Sidd-as-Sahba, and he married her after she became clean of her menstrual cycle.

1764 At Khaybar Mohammed instituted the first dhimmis. A dhimmi agrees to live under the Sharia [Islamic law] and give up all political power. After the best of the goods were taken from the Jews, Mohammed left them to work the land. Since his men knew nothing about farming, and the Jews were skilled at it, they worked the land and gave Mohammed half of their profits.

♀ 1765 After Mohammed rested, the wife of Sallam prepared a meal for him. She asked which piece of meat he preferred and gave it to him. He chewed a bite and spit it out and declared it to be poisoned. He asked the Jewess about this and she agreed it was poisoned. She said that after what he had done to other Jews, she wanted to rid herself of him if he were only a king. If he were a prophet, he would know not to eat it. The Muslim at the table with Mohammed did not spit his meat out and he died.

♀ 1767 It was time for Safiya's wedding, so she was 'beautified' by a Muslim for her wedding night with Mohammed. When Mohammed awoke in the morning he found a young Muslim walking around his tent with a drawn sword. He asked what he was doing. He said, "I was afraid for you. You killed her husband, tortured her father to death, and destroyed her people." Mohammed asked Allah to preserve the fighter as well as he preserved Mohammed.

♀ 1768 Mohammed gave the jihadi women a small share of the booty. He gave a portion of Khaybar to his wives as well.

FADAK

1777 The Jews of Fadak panicked when they saw what Mohammed did at Khaybar. They would be next, so they surrendered to Mohammed without a fight. Since there was no battle Mohammed got all of their goods and they worked the land and gave half to Mohammed each year. They became dhimmis like those of Khaybar. They could still be Jews, but they gave up all power. This is Islamic tolerance of other religions.

This is the Sunna of Mohammed

MOHAMMED'S FINAL JIHAD

CHAPTER 13

*"Our Lord! We believe in what Thou hast revealed,
and we follow the Apostle; then write us down among
those who bear witness."* [Koran 3:53]

MECCA CONQUERED

The treaty of Hudaybiya was broken by a fight between allies of Mohammed and allies of Mecca. Mohammed took advantage of this and attacked Mecca.

1810 A Muslim of Medina, Hatib, wrote a letter to the Meccans saying 𝖰 that Mohammed was coming to Mecca. He then paid a woman to take the letter to Mecca. She concealed the letter in her hair. Mohammed received information that she was carrying the letter and sent two men after her. They caught up with her, searched her and found nothing. Ali ordered her to produce the letter or they would strip her naked. She gave them the letter.

1810 When they returned to Medina, Mohammed called for Hatib and demanded an answer. He said that he was not a man of importance and he was just trying to take care of family left in Mecca. Umar wanted to behead him, but Mohammed pointed out that Hatib had fought at Badr and could do as he pleased.

1811 As a result of the fighting between a tribe allied with the Meccans and a tribe allied with him, Mohammed marched on Mecca with 10,000 men to punish them.

The Meccans decided to yield without a fight. The Meccan leader submitted to Islam. The leader went ahead and announced to the citizens that Mohammed's army was coming. They were not to resist but to go into their houses, his house or the Kabah and that they would be safe.

1819 Mohammed had told his commanders only to kill those who resisted. Otherwise they were to bother no one except for those who had spoken against Mohammed. The list of those to be killed:

- One of Mohammed's secretaries, who had said that when he was recording Mohammed's Koranic revelations sometimes Mohammed let the secretary insert better speech. This caused him to lose faith and he became an apostate (left Islam).
- Two singing girls who had sung satires against Mohammed.
- A Muslim tax collector who had become an apostate.
- A man who had insulted Mohammed.

♀ T1642 Hind was the Meccan woman who had mutilated Hamza at the battle of Uhud. When she came before Mohammed to become a Muslim, he told her that her duties included not killing children. She replied that she had raised them and not killed them. But when the sons were grown Mohammed had killed both of them at Badr.

1821 Mohammed went to the Kabah, the cube-shaped sacred site, prayed and then destroyed all of the religious art in Mecca.

Mohammed announced the end of all feuds, all revenge killings, and payment of blood money. Veneration of the ancestors was over.

KHALID'S EXPEDITIONS

1834 Mohammed sent Khalid out to the tribes around the Meccan countryside.

♀ 1837 Khalid attacked one tribe, bound and beheaded many of them. One of those who was tied asked to be taken over to a girl. The man said, "Good bye, though life is at an end." He then quoted a love poem to her:

> Was I not a worthy lover?
> Did I not undertake journeys day and night for you?
> Reward me with love before tragedy
> Reward me with love before the distance is too great
> Even when our tribe's troubles took my attention
> Even then my love was there.

♀ 1838 She replied, "May your life be lengthened for years." He was taken away and beheaded.

1840 Mohammed sent Khalid to an ancient temple near Mecca that was used by several tribes for worship. When Khalid got there, he destroyed it completely.

THE BATTLE OF HUNAIN

1840 When Mohammed took Mecca, the surrounding Arab tribes saw that if he were not opposed, he would become King of Arabia. The Hawazin Arabs decided to oppose him under the leadership of Malik.

1842 Mohammed sent a spy to gather intelligence about the Arabs. When he received the information, he began preparing for jihad. He first borrowed armor and lances from a wealthy Meccan and then marched out with 12,000 men.

1845 The army descended into a broad area and they found the enemy prepared and hiding, waiting to attack. The Muslim troops broke and ran.

Mohammed stood in his stirrups and called out, "Where are you going? Come to me, the Apostle of Allah." Most of the men continued to retreat except his battle-hardened core troops who regrouped around him. A group of about 100 led the charge to turn the tide. They were steadfast. Mohammed looked at the carnage and said, "Now the oven is hot!"

1847 One of the Muslim women was near Mohammed and said about ♀ those who were retreating, "Kill those who flee just as you kill those who are attacking us."

Once again, Islam defeated the Kafirs.

BATTLE OF TAIF

1872 Mohammed attacked al Taif, a walled town. The Muslims pitched their tents near the walls and settled down for a siege. Mohammed had brought two wives and put them into two tents. The battle did not go well and the town was successful in resisting jihad. Mohammed had the fighters destroy all of their vineyards.

1873 One of the Muslim women asked Mohammed if she could have the ♀ jewelry of two of the richest women in Taif. Mohammed said she could but ♂ he doubted that they were going to succeed. Shortly after that he called off the attack. On the way back, one of the Muslims said that he did not mind losing the battle, but he did regret not getting a woman from Taif for a slave. The people of Taif were noted for their intelligence and he wanted to breed the slave to have smart children from her.

THE HAWAZIN

1877 The Hawazin had been beaten by the Muslims. As Mohammed came back from Taif, he stopped to deal with them. They had submitted to Islam and wanted relief from their loss. Their leaders pointed out to Mohammed that some of his prisoners were members of his foster family. Mohammed gave the leaders a choice. They could have their cattle and goods back or their wives and sons back. They choose their families.

1877 Mohammed asked the various tribal leaders of his army if they ♀ would turn the Hawazin loose. Most of them did, but two tribes said no, so Mohammed offered them six camels for each person they freed. The debt would be paid from the next battle. They then freed all of the captives, but one. One of the captors had a old woman that he did want to free for six camels. He thought that she was rich and worth more. His friend said, "Let her go. Her breasts are flat. She can't conceive and her mouth is cold. It is not like she is a virgin in her prime or even a plump middle-aged matron." He let her go for six camels.

♀
♂ 1878 Mohammed gave three of his companions a slave girl for each to use for sex. Uthman took his sex slave and gave her to his son.

THE RAID ON TABUK

1894 Mohammed decided to raid the Byzantines. Normally he never let his men actually know where he was headed. He would not announce a destination until they were on the way, he would announce the actual target. This raid was far away and the weather was very hot, so greater preparations had to be made. The men began to prepare, but with no enthusiasm because of the heat. It was time for the harvest to begin, and they remembered the last combat with the Byzantines where they lost badly.

♀ 1894 When Mohammed asked one of his best men if he wanted to go, the man replied, "Would you allow me to stay? You know how much I love women and when I see the Byzantine women, I don't know if I will be able to control myself." So Mohammed told him to stay.

1896 So Mohammed set off, but there were many Muslims who were slow to leave or they came with misgivings. After the first camp some of the Muslims left and returned to Medina. They were called hypocrites.

1902 When they got to Tabuk, the people there paid the poll tax, *jizya* [a tax paid by Kafirs]. By paying the poll tax, a per-person tax, they would not be attacked, killed or robbed by the Muslims. Those who paid the jizya were under the protection of Islam This is what is meant by tolerance in Islam.

1903 Mohammed sent Khalid to the fort of a Christian chief. When the chief and his brother rode out of their fort to inspect the cattle, Khalid killed the chief's brother and captured the ruler. The chief agreed to pay the poll tax to Islam. Mohammed returned to Medina.

ETERNAL JIHAD

M448 After all the victories, some Muslims said that the days of fighting were over and even began to sell their arms. But Mohammed forbid this, saying, "There shall not cease from the midst of my people a party engaged in fighting for the truth, until the Antichrist appears." Jihad was recognized as the normal state of affairs.

ABU BAKR LEADS THE PILGRIMAGE

1919-20 Abu Bakr led the pilgrimage from Medina to Mecca. While they were in Mecca, major changes were made to the treaty of Hudaybiya, which are recorded in the Koran. The treaty was only to be good for four more months, then jihad would be declared if the Kafirs didn't submit to Islam.

1922 After this time, those who practiced the old native religions of Arabia would no longer be able to go to Mecca for pilgrimage.

1924 Because the Kafirs are considered unclean, they could not approach the Kabah. The money lost from their pilgrimages would be taken care of by Allah. Jihad would bring in the lost money.

1933 When Mohammed had taken Mecca and Tabuk, deputations began to come from the Arabs. The Arabs were waiting to see what would happen between the Quraysh and Mohammed. When Mohammed was victorious, the Arabs came in groups and joined with him.

1956 The kings of Himyar wrote to Mohammed that they had submitted to Islam. Mohammed wrote them back, "... I received your message and am informed of your conversion to Islam and your killing Kafirs. Allah has guided you. ... send the one-fifth of the spoils of war and tax the believers... Christians and Jews who do not convert must pay the poll tax ..."

1957 Mohammed sent Muadh to Yemen to proselytize. While he was ♀ there a woman asked what rights a husband has over his wife. He replied to the woman who asked, "If you went home and found your husband's nose running with pus and blood and you sucked it until it was cleaned, you still would not have fulfilled your husband's rights."

1965 Mohammed sent out tax collectors to every part of Islam to collect the tax.

This is the Sunna of Mohammed

MOHAMMED'S LAST YEAR

CHAPTER 14

But when Allah and His Messenger call the true
believers to judge between them, their response is, "We
have heard, and we obey." [Koran 24:51]

THE FAREWELL PILGRIMAGE

♀ 1966 Mohammed took Aisha with him on the pilgrimage to Mecca. However, Aisha's menstrual period had started and she was unclean. So she started to cry, but Mohammed said that she could observe all of the rituals except for going around the Kabah.

1968 Ten years after entering Medina, Mohammed made what was to be his last pilgrimage to Mecca. There he made his farewell address:

♀ 1969 The men have rights over their wives and the wives have rights over the men. The wives must never commit adultery nor act in a sexual manner towards others. If they do, put them in separate rooms and beat them lightly. If they refrain from these things, they have the right to food and clothing. Lay injunctions on women lightly for they are prisoners of the men and have no control over their persons.

⚧ M473 Feed and clothe your slaves well.

THE FINAL STATE OF CHRISTIANS AND JEWS

M453 When Mohammed first started preaching in Mecca, his religion was Arabian. Then the god defined by the Koran became identified with god of the Torah and other Jewish elements were introduced. When Mohammed moved to Medina, he argued with the Jews when they denied his status as a prophet in the Judaic line. He then annihilated the Jews.

M453 In his last statement, Jews and Christians became perpetual second class political citizens, dhimmis. Only those Christians and Jews who submit to Islam are protected. The real Christians are those who deny the Trinity and accept Mohammed as the final prophet. The real Jews are those who accept Mohammed as the final prophet of their god, Jehovah. Both Christians and Jews must accept that the Koran is the true Scripture and that the Old Testament and New Testament are corrupt and in error. All other Jews and Christians are false and Kafirs.

Koran 9:29 *Make war on those who have received the Scriptures [Jews and Christians] but do not believe in Allah or in the Last Day. They do not forbid what Allah and His Messenger have forbidden. The Christians and Jews do not follow the religion of truth until they submit and pay the poll tax [jizya], and they are humiliated.*

The Christians have hidden their prophesies that Mohammed would come to fulfill the work of Christ. To believe in the divinity of Christ is to refuse to submit to Islam. Like the Jews, only those Christians who submit to Islam, honor Mohammed as their last prophet, become dhimmis and are ruled by the Sharia (Islamic law) are actual Christians. Islam defines all religions. All religions must submit to Islam.

SUMMARY OF MOHAMMED'S ARMED EVENTS

1973 In a nine year period Mohammed personally took part in twenty-seven raids. There were thirty-eight other battles and expeditions. This is a total of sixty-five armed events, not including assassinations and executions, for an average of one armed event every six weeks.

MOHAMMED'S DEATH

I1000 When Mohammed spoke to Aisha, his favorite wife, she complained ♀ of a headache. Mohammed said, "No, Aisha, Oh my head. Would it distress you if you were to die before me so that I might wrap you in your shroud and pray over you?" Aisha said, "I think that if you did that, that after you returned to the house you would simply spend the night with one of your other wives." But the pain became worse and he took his final illness in the house of Aisha.

I1006 Mohammed weakened and was in a great deal of pain. Later he died ♀ with his head in Aisha's lap. His final words were the perfect summation of Islam, political action based upon religion.

B4,52,288 *Mohammed said, "There should be no other religions besides Islam in Arabia" and that money should continue to be paid to influence the foreign, Kafir ambassadors.*

T1831 Mohammed was buried beneath his bed. The bed was removed and a grave was dug where it had stood.

This is the Sunna of Mohammed

MOHAMMED, THE MAN

Chapter 15

*So obey Allah and His messenger. But if you turn your
backs to them, Our messenger is not to blame, for his duty
is only to deliver Our warning clearly.* [Koran 64:12]

HIS PHYSICAL APPEARANCE

B5,58,280 Pagans would part their hair, but Mohammed used to wear his
hair falling loose like the people of the Scriptures [the Jews]. If not instructed
differently, Mohammed would follow their example. Later, however, Mohammed began to wear his hair parted.

B7,72,787 Mohammed was neither tall nor short. His complexion was
similarly muted, neither pale nor bronzed. His hair was not particularly curly
or straight. He became Allah's Apostle at forty, spending ten years in Mecca
and ten years at Medina. He died at the age of sixty.

B7,72,791 Qatada asked Anas to describe Mohammed's hair. Anas said,
"Mohammed's hair reached almost to his shoulders. It was wavy. Not straight,
but not very curly, either.

B7,72,793 Mohammed had a unique look to him. He had big feet and hands,
but his palms were soft.

B4,56,751 Mohammed was of average height and had wide shoulders and
long hair. I saw him wearing a red cloak one time, and I thought he was the
most handsome man I had ever seen.

MOHAMMED'S WHITENESS

There are many hadiths that report Mohammed's whiteness.

B4,56,765 When Mohammed prostrated himself to pray, he would spread
his arms so wide apart, that we could see his armpits. Ibn Bukair described
it as "the whiteness of his armpits."

B9,90,342 At the battle of Al-Ahzab, Mohammed helped us carry dirt to the
fortifications. We could see the dust covering his white belly.

B1,3,63 We were sitting with Mohammed in the Mosque one day when a
man rode up on a camel. He asked, "Which one of you is Mohammed?" We
answered, "That white man leaning on his arm…"

B1,8,367 Just before the battle of Khaybar, we and Mohammed gave the Fajr prayer before sunup. I [Anas] was riding behind Abu Talha and next to Mohammed. We were so close, that as we rode down the main street of Khaybar, my knee touched Mohammed's leg. His garment moved and exposed the whiteness of his thigh.

B4,56,747 Rabia Bin Abi Abdur-Rahman heard Anas Bin Malik describe Mohammed like this: "For our people, he was average height. Not tall, but not short. He had an middling complexion, rosy, not pale white, but not dark brown either. His hair was wavy: not very curly, but not very straight. Allah first spoke to him when he was forty. He received Allah's revelations for ten years while in Mecca. He then stayed in Medina for another ten years. When he died, he had maybe twenty gray hairs on his head and in his beard." Rabia said, "One time I saw some of his hair and it was red. I was told that perfume had turned it red."

HIS ANGER

There are many hadiths about Mohammed's anger.

B1,2,19 If Mohammed ordered a Muslim to do something, he made sure that it was something that was easily done, something within their limits of strength or endurance. Still, many complained, "Mohammed, we can't do that. We are not like you. Allah has freed you from all sin." The anger was apparent on Mohammed's face and he said, "No one fears Allah more than I, and I know Allah better than any of you."

B1,3,90 A man once said to Mohammed, "I may not be able to go to the obligatory prayer because our Imam is very long-winded when he leads the ceremony." The narrator continued, "I had never seen Mohammed more angry. He said, 'Some of you are making the others dislike praying. If you lead the prayers, then you should keep it brief. Some of the people are sick, weak, or simply have work to do.'"

HIS CURSES

B9,85,73 Mohammed would beseech Allah in this prayer, "Allah, Save the weak Muslims. Be cruel to the Mudar and smite them with years of famine and hunger just as you brought famine to the people during the time of Joseph."

HIS WIFE AISHA

Aisha was his favorite wife. This dream occurred when she was six.

M031,5977 Aisha quotes Mohammed: "Three nights in a row I saw you in a dream. An angel delivered you wrapped in silks and said, 'This is your wife.' As I unwrapped the silk, your face appeared. I said, 'If this dream is indeed from Allah, then let Him make it happen.'"

M008,3309 Mohammed and I [Aisha] were married when I was six. I was brought to his house when I was nine. We moved to Medina where I fell sick with a fever for a month. My hair fell out as a result of the illness. My mother, Umm Ruman, came for me one day as I was playing on a swing with some friends. I had no idea what she wanted, but she took me by the hand and had me stand by the door of our house. I was out of breath, but when I had composed myself, my mother took me inside and handed me over to some of the Helper women who proceeded to wish me good luck. The women washed me and made me pretty. Mohammed came in the morning and I was given to him.

B8,73,151 My girl friends and I [Aisha] would play with dolls while in Mohammed's presence. They would try to hide when he entered, but he always would call them back to play with me. Playing with dolls or anything with a human image was forbidden, but because I was so young, not yet having reached puberty, it was allowed.

HIS OTHER WIVES

B3,47,755 The wives of Mohammed collected themselves in two groups. The first group consisted of Aisha, Haifsa, Safiya, and Sauda. The other group was made up of Um Salama and his other wives. The Muslims all knew that Mohammed loved Aisha, so if someone had a gift to give Mohammed, they would wait until he was staying at her home.

This made the wives in Um Salama's group jealous and they sent Um Salama to the prophet to request that he tell the people to send their gifts to him in whoever's house he happened to be in. Um Salama made the request to Mohammed several times, each time getting no reply. Finally, he answered her by saying, "Do not try to hurt me on Aisha's account. Allah's revelations do not come to me when I am not in her bed." Um Salama said to him, "I apologize to Allah for causing you pain."

The wives remained unhappy, so they sent Mohammed's daughter, Fatima, to him. Fatima said to Mohammed, "Your wives ask that you treat them as well as you do Abu Bakr's daughter, Aisha." Mohammed said to her, "Do you love what I love?" She said that she did, and when the jealous wives asked her to intercede with her father again, she refused.

Finally, they sent Zainab to him. Zainab was bitter and spoke harshly as she asked that Aisha be shown no favoritism. Zainab began to shout and scold and abuse Aisha to her face. Aisha then vigorously answered Zainab's complaints until she was left silent. Mohammed looked at Aisha and said, "She is certainly Abu Bakr's daughter."

SEX

B1,5,249 Narrated by Maimuna, a wife of Mohammed: After sex, Mohammed purified himself just as he would for prayer except that he would not wash his feet. He would rinse off the semen and vaginal secretions from his penis and then pour water over the rest of his body. He would then remove his feet from the bathtub and wash them. That was how Mohammed cleaned himself after sex.

B1,6,298 Mohammed and I [Aisha] would bathe together after sex in the same tub. During my period, he would have me wear a dress that only covered me from the waist down and he would fondle me. He would also let me wash his head while I was menstruating.

HABITS

B4,54,428 Aisha said that Mohammed would become very agitated if he saw a cloud in the sky. He would pace back and forth, continually enter and exit his house and his face would change color. If it rained, however, he would become relaxed. Aisha always recognized that mood of his. When she asked about it he said, "I don't know why I'm afraid. It might be the same agitation that the people of Ad referred to in the Koran:

> Koran 46:24 *Then they saw a cloud coming into their valley. They said, "The cloud is bringing us rain." No, it is the scourge you sought, a wind that carries agonizing retribution. Everything was destroyed by the command of the Lord. Morning rose on empty houses—the reward of the guilty.*

B7,65,292 Mohammed preferred to begin things from the right side; combing his hair, putting on his shoes, or performing ablution. He would follow this practice in every thing he did.

M023,5018 Anas said that Mohammed forbade people to drink while standing. Qatada related: We asked him, "What about eating while standing?" Anas said, "That is even more objectionable."

M023,5029 Anas related the story that Mohammed would drink his refreshments in three gulps.

M023,5037 Mohammed: "When a Muslim eats, they should not wipe their hand until it is licked clean, either by themselves or by someone else."

M024,5231 Mohammed: "When someone puts on sandals, he should put the right one on first. When someone takes off sandals, he should take off the left one first. Either this or simply put them on or take them off at the same time."

M024,5234 Mohammed made it illegal for a man to eat with his left hand or walk with only one sandal on. He also forbade a man to wear a garment that had no opening for the arms to extend or support himself when wearing a single garment that might expose his genitalia.

M024,5238 Mohammed: "No one should lie on his back with one foot placed on top of the other."

MODESTY

B7,72,807 One day a man peeped into Mohammed's house and saw him scratching his head with a comb. Noticing the man Mohammed said, "If I had realized that you were peeking at me I would have stuck this comb in your eye. The reason that people must ask permission is to keep them from seeing things that they shouldn't."

MOHAMMED'S SLAVES

The woman that Mohammed's "right hand possessed" was a captive used as a slave for his pleasure in sex.

B9,89,321 Mohammed would only take a pledge of allegiance from a woman if she first recited this Koranic verse:

Koran 60:12 *O, Messenger, when believing women come to you and pledge an oath of allegiance to you and ascribe no other gods as partners to Allah ...*

Mohammed would never allow his hand to touch a woman's hand unless she was a woman that his right hand possessed, that is his slave or one of his wives slaves.

B3,34,351 A man committed himself to freeing one of his slaves upon his death, but later needed money. Mohammed took the slave and asked, "Does anyone want to buy this slave from me?" Nu Aim received the slave from Mohammed after giving the Prophet a certain price.

B3,46,717 I, Ibn Aun, wrote Nafi a letter, and his reply said that the forces of Mohammed had initiated a surprise attack on the Bani Mustaliq when they were watering their cattle and not paying attention. Their men were slain and their women and children were seized. A woman, Juwairiya, was given to Mohammed as spoils of war that day. Nafi's letter said that he had heard the account from Ibn Umar, who was in the attacking army that day.

B3,47,765 Narrated by Kurib, a freed slave of Ibn Abbas: "Maimuna, one of the Prophet's wives, told me one day that she had freed one of her slave girls without first asking Mohammed's permission. When it was her turn to stay with Mohammed, she said, 'Are you aware that I have freed my slave girl?' He replied, 'Really?' 'Yes,' she said. Mohammed said, 'Your reward would have been greater if you had given her to one of your mother's brothers.'"

B7,65,344 While at the house of his slave tailor, Mohammed ate a gourd dish that he seemed to enjoy. Ever since then, I [Anas] have enjoyed eating gourd.

B9,91,368 Umar sought Mohammed and found him in an upstairs room with a black slave standing guard at the top of the stairs. Umar said to the slave, "Inform Mohammed that Umar is here and seeks permission to see him." The slave then admitted me to the room.

WAR

Mohammed was devoted to violence in the cause of Islam.

B9,90,332 Abu Huraira overheard Mohammed say, "By Allah, if I had a way of transporting all the men who wished to fight in jihad, I would not miss any opportunity to fight the Kafir. It would be a pleasure to be martyred for Allah, be resurrected, and martyred again and again."

B4,52,151 Mohammed and Abu Talha would share a shield in battle. Abu Talha was an exceptional archer, and Mohammed would follow the flight of his arrows as they sped toward their target.

Humor in jihad.

M031,5932 Amir B. Sa'd reported, on the authority of his father, that Allah's Apostle gathered his parents for him on the Day of Uhud when a polytheist had set fire to (i.e. attacked fiercely) the Muslims. Thereupon Allah's Apostle said to him: "(Sa'd), shoot an arrow, (Sa'd), may my mother and father be taken as ransom for you." I drew an arrow and I shot a featherless arrow at the Meccan polytheist, aiming his side. He fell down and his private parts were exposed. Allah's Messenger laughed so that I saw his front teeth.

CRUELTY

B2,24,577 Some people came to Medina, but the climate made them sick, so Mohammed gave them permission to stay among the camels that had been collected for taxes. He told them to drink the camel's urine and milk, as that would cure their illness. However, the people instead murdered the shepherd and stole the camels. Mohammed sent men after them and they were quickly captured. Mohammed ordered that their hands and feet be cut off, and their eyes pierced with hot pokers. They were left to die of thirst on the rocks of Harra.

HIS BODILY FUNCTIONS

One of many hadiths about Mohammed and elimination.

B1,9,479 Whenever Mohammed went to the toilet, another boy and I would follow with a stick, a staff and a container of water. When he finished, we would give him the water.

This is the Sunna of Mohammed

THE TEARS OF JIHAD

CHAPTER 16

These figures are a rough estimate of the death of Kafirs by the political act of jihad found in the Koran, Sira and Hadith.

AFRICANS

Thomas Sowell estimates that 11 million slaves were shipped across the Atlantic and 14 million were sent to the Islamic nations of North Africa and the Middle East.[1] For every slave captured, many others died. Estimates of this collateral damage vary. The renowned missionary David Livingstone estimated that for every slave who reached the plantation, five others died by being killed in the raid or died on the forced march from illness and privation.[2] So, for 25 million slaves delivered to the market, we have the death of about 120 million people. Islam ran the wholesale slave trade in Africa.[3]

120 million Africans

CHRISTIANS

The number of Christians martyred by Islam is 9 million.[4] A rough estimate by Raphael Moore in *History of Asia Minor* is that another 50 million died in wars by jihad. So to account for the 1 million African Christians killed in the 20th century we have:

60 million Christians

JEWS

The Jews had no political control over any country, and their deaths were limited to a few thousand killed in riots.

---

1. Thomas Sowell, *Race and Culture* (New York: Basic Books, 1994), 188.
2. J. H. Worcester, *Life of David Livingstone* (Chicago: Woman's Presbyterian Board of Missions, 1888), 62.
3. Bernard Lewis, *Race and Slavery in the Middle East* (New York: Oxford University Press, 1990).
4. David B. Barrett, Todd M. Johnson, *World Christian Trends AD 30-AD 2200* (Pasadena: William Carey Library, 2001), 230, table 4-10.

HINDUS

Koenard Elst in *Negationism in India*[5] gives an estimate of 80 million Hindus killed in the total jihad against India. The country of India today is only half the size of ancient India, due to jihad. The mountains near India are called the Hindu Kush, meaning the "funeral pyre of the Hindus."

80 million Hindus

BUDDHISTS

Buddhists do not keep up with the history of war. Keep in mind that in jihad, only Christians and Jews were allowed to survive as dhimmis (second-class subjects under Sharia); everyone else had to convert or die. Jihad killed the Buddhists in Turkey, Afghanistan, along the Silk Route, and in India. The total is roughly 10 million.[6]

10 million Buddhists

TOTAL

This gives a rough estimate of *270 million* killed by jihad.

---

5. Koenard Elst, *Negationism in India* (New Delhi: Voice of India, 2002), 34.
6. Barrett and Johnson, *World Christian Trends AD 30-AD 2200,* 230, table 4-1.

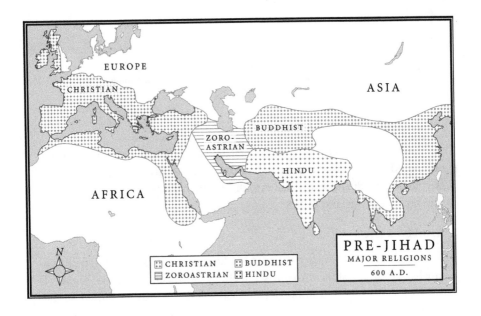

PRE-JIHAD
MAJOR RELIGIONS
600 A.D.

CHRISTIAN BUDDHIST
ZOROASTRIAN HINDU

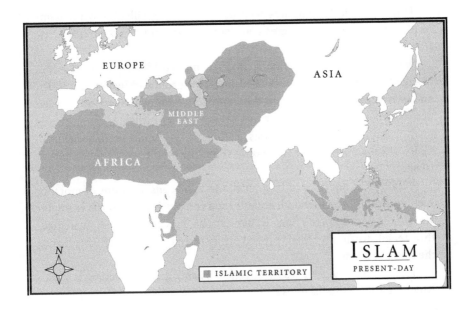

ISLAM
PRESENT-DAY

ISLAMIC TERRITORY

COMMENTS

Our Lord! We believe in what Thou hast revealed, and we follow the Apostle; then write us down among those who bear witness. [Koran 3:53]

SUBMISSION AND DUALITY

After Mohammed declared himself to be the messenger of Allah, he advanced the idea that everyone had to submit to his message. His entire world became dualistic, divided into those who believed him and those who did not—believers and Kafirs.

DUAL ETHICS

Islam's success came in politics in Medina. His politics were based upon a dualistic ethical system with one set of ethics for Muslims and another set of ethics for Kafirs. An example of this duality is that a Muslim should not lie to another Muslim, but on several occasions Mohammed gave permission to lie to Kafirs to advance the cause of Allah.

This dual ethical system was necessary to implement jihad, and it remains in place today. Dual ethics create an "other" that can be treated differently from a Muslim.

When Mohammed became a prophet, his world-view and his ethics changed. Humanity became divided into two groups—Muslim and Kafir, and he treated these two groups differently. Mohammed's reactions to each person depended upon whether that person was a Muslim.

Mohammed's political view was profoundly and fundamentally dualistic. Unity of humanity would come only when the whole world submitted to Islam.

A Kafir does not have to be granted the usual considerations of morality such as equality, brotherhood, honesty, and compassion. From the examples we see in Mohammed's life, Kafirs can be mocked, cursed, maligned, threatened, tortured, killed, robbed, assassinated, or enslaved to advance the cause of Islam.

If an action against a Kafir advances Islam, then the action is good. Anything that resists Islam is evil.

JIHAD

Jihad is dual ethics with sacred violence. The Koran calls the jihad of the sword, fighting in Allah's cause. But jihad is also waged with speech, writing and money. The key religious element of the dual ethics is that Allah sanctifies violence for complete domination. The Kafirs must submit to Islam.

Jihad is usually called "holy war" but this is far too narrow a view. Jihad means struggle or effort and is a process that is epitomized by the life of Mohammed, the perfect jihadist. In Mecca, Mohammed demonstrated the initial practice of jihad when Islam was weak: persuasion and conversion. When he moved to Medina, he demonstrated how jihad worked when Islam was strong: using immigration against inhabitants, creating political power by struggling against the host, dominating other religions, using violence, and establishing a government.

All of the Trilogy deals with jihad.[1]

AMOUNT OF TRILOGY TEXT DEVOTED TO JIHAD

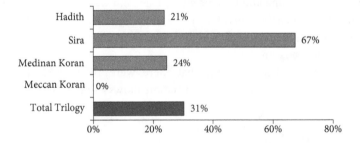

THE JIHAD OF MECCA

From the standpoint of war, jihad did not begin until Mohammed's first killing attack in Medina. But its roots go back to Mecca when Mohammed cursed the ancient native Arabic gods. Jihad is a force that manifests itself according to circumstances. The violence may go no further than aggressive arguments, beatings, put-downs, hostility, insults, or threats, but it is always based upon an ethical system of duality that started in Mecca.

In Mecca, Mohammed promised his critics' slaughter. When heated arguments broke out between the Meccans and Muslims, it was a Muslim who picked up a weapon and drew blood. It was a Muslim, Umar, who violently protested over a poem. Mohammed was in Mecca when he signed

---

1   For more information on statistics and methods used: https://www.politicalislam.com/trilogy-project

a blood oath with the Muslims of Medina. The root of the violence of Medina was the peace of Mecca. There was no killing of Kafirs in Mecca, but the Kafir was lower than an animal. Allah hates the Kafir. The peace of Mecca included hate. It was a peace that demanded submission.

THE SUCCESS OF POLITICAL ISLAM AND JIHAD

It is possible to take the data found in the Sira and give a scientific basis for the success of Islam.

Religious Islam is defined as doctrine concerned with going to Paradise and avoiding Hell by following the Koran and the Sunna. The part of Islam that deals with the "outsider", the Kafir, is defined as political Islam. Since so much of the Trilogy is about the Kafir, the statistical conclusion is that Islam is primarily a political system, not a religious system. Mohammed's success depended on politics, not religion. The Sira, Mohammed's biography, gives a highly detailed accounting of his rise to power. He preached the religion of Islam for 13 years in Mecca and garnered 150 followers. He was forced to move to Medina and became a politician and warrior. During the last 9 years of his life, he was involved in 95 violent events. When he died, nearly every Arab in the peninsula was a Muslim. Mohammed succeeded through politics, not religion.

An estimate can be made that there were 100,000 Muslims when Mohammed died.[2] Using this information allows a graph to be drawn:

GROWTH OF ISLAM

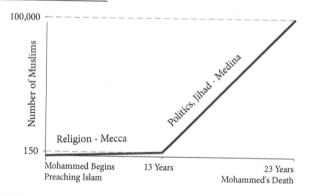

---

2   *The History of al-Tabari*, volume XI (Albany, NY: SUNY), page 9. Khalid, the sword of Allah, went into battle in 633 AD (Mohammed died in 632 AD), with 10,000 Muslim Arab troops at the Battle of Chains. A nation at full conflict can field an army of about 10% of its population. If 10% is 10,000, then the total population is 100,000. This is a very rough estimate.

There are two distinct growth processes—religion and politics. Teaching and religion grew at a rate of about 12 new Muslims per year. Politics and jihad grew at a rate of 10,000 new Muslims per year, an enormous increase. Politics was almost a thousand times more effective than religion.

There would be no Islam today, if it were only a religion. Statistics show that Islamic politics is what brought Islam success, not religion. To say that Islam is the religion of peace misses the point, since the religion is not the core of Islam's power. It is its politics that bring success, not its religion.

The statistical conclusion: Islam is primarily a political ideology.

THE SUPREME MASTER OF CIVILIZATIONAL WAR

Mohammed was the supreme master of civilizational war and has had no equal to this day. His understanding of the use of force was sophisticated and subtle. Physical violence was only a small part of his understanding of war.

Mohammed's profound insight was not simply the waging of physical war but of waging war of the mind, emotions, culture, politics, and religion. There is no aspect of being human that Mohammed did not use for war. Money, salvation, sex, culture, religion, destiny, family, immigration, legal codes, government, power, deceit, racial pride, tribalism, community, fear, propaganda, diplomacy, spy-craft, philosophy, ethics, and psychology were all used for jihad. Jihad was not holy war but complete and total civilizational war.

ISLAMIZATION OF A CULTURE

The Sira gives a dynamic picture of how Islam enters a culture. When Mohammed started preaching in Mecca, there was no animosity. Islam was portrayed as a logical continuation of the native Arabic religions. Then Islam claimed to be a "brother religion" to Judaism. Next it claimed not just to be a better religion but the best, and all of the other religions were wrong. Islam was publicly confrontational, attacking every aspect of the host culture. Hostility developed between Islam and the Meccan culture of religious tolerance. The Meccans tried to placate the Muslims, but there could be no compromise. Islam turned increasingly to violence that culminated in a treaty of war with new allies in Medina.

When the Muslims immigrated to Medina, the migrants were peaceful. But when the Jews said that Mohammed was not a prophet in the Jewish tradition, Islam became hostile. Islam was the better religion; and if debate did not show that, then forceful arguments would. Up to this point, the process of Islam in Medina was the same as in Mecca.

In Medina Mohammed found a way to obtain money and settle old scores with the Meccans who had never submitted to Islam. The solution was political—jihad against the Meccans, the Jews, and their neighbors. By jihad, political Islam conquered all of Arabia in nine years.

MOHAMMED AND THE JEWS

The relationship between Mohammed and the Jews takes up a very large part of the Sira. In Mecca, Mohammed's relationship with them was religious. Mohammed identified Allah with Jehovah. (Mohammed never explained who Allah was. He did not have to. Allah, the moon god, was chief of the many gods in the Kabah. The Quraysh tribe swore all oaths by Allah long before Mohammed did.) The Koran adopted the Jewish stories about Moses, Adam, and others to make the point that Allah would punish those who didn't obey His prophets.

He took this stance when he was in Mecca where there were very few Jews. In contrast, Medina was about half Jewish. Their leaders were weak debaters but, even so, they let Mohammed know he was not a Jewish prophet. The tone of Mohammed and the Koran then changed regarding Jews. The theological ground was laid for their destruction.

The first two tribes had the choice of conversion or exile and losing their possessions. But the third tribe of Medina had the choice of conversion or death. The Jews of Khaybar had the choice of conversion or dhimmitude, a permanent second-class legal status.

The Trilogy[3] is even more negative about the Jews than Hitler's *Mein Kampf.*

ANTI-JEWISH TEXT IN TRILOGY

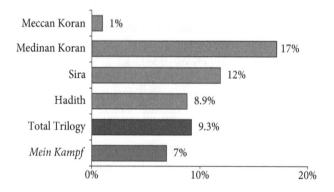

---

3   For more information on statistics and methods used: https://www. politicalislam.com/trilogy-project

DHIMMIS

The relationship between Islam the Christians and Jews was formed by Mohammed. The relationship is the dhimmi status, or dhimmitude, as established at Khaybar after the Jews were crushed. A dhimmi is a Jew or Christian who agrees to be a second-class subject politically, culturally, and religiously. The dhimmi sacrifices all civil rights and pays a special tax of humiliation. Indeed, the cash flow of the empire of Islam was based upon this special tax, the *jizya*.

SLAVERY

Mohammed captured slaves, sold slaves, bought slaves, freed slaves, tortured slaves, had sex with slaves, gave slaves as gifts of pleasure, received slaves as gifts, and used slaves for work. In Islam, slavery is a blessing. Either the slave or his family will one day convert to Islam in order to be freed, thereby creating new Muslims.

A WAR OF CIVILIZATIONS

Islam is a civilization of dualism and submission. Our civilization has the ideals of a unitary ethics and freedom. Equality and freedom have no basis in duality and submission. You can't submit and be free. There is no equality in submission.

For 1,400 years Islam has triumphed over the Kafir. Once we understand the true nature of the civilization of Islam, we can defeat dualism and triumph over submission.

TRANSLATING THE KORAN INTO ENGLISH

The Koran contains a problematic mixture of beauty, violence and obscurity. One of the proposed solutions to the problems of the Koran is that a "better" translation can eliminate the problem of the horrendous violence.

There have been two approaches to the translation of the violence—reveal the violence or soften the violence. You can see the two approaches in web sites that produce parallel translations. One example is http://www.quranbrowser.com/ which gives ten translations, or the http://corpus.quran.com/ which provides an original Arabic version.

Whatever translation is used, it must match the story found in the Sira, the sacred biography of Mohammed, and the Hadith, his traditions. Both the Sira and the Hadith are filled with violent jihad, so the harsh translation version of the Koran matches the historic jihad doctrine found in Mohammed's life.

The CSPI Korans clarify the effect of the Koran on Kafirs, non-Muslims. This means that subtle religious doctrine is secondary. The CSPI point of view is that of the Kafir, the outsider. The CSPI versions enable anyone to understand the Korans found in a bookstore.

Here is a list of the primary references used in producing the CSPI Korans:

- Ali, Maulana Muhammad. *Holy Koran* (Columbus, Ohio: Ahmadiyyah Anjuman Ishaat Islam, 1998).
- Arberry, A. J. *The Koran Interpreted* (New York: Touchstone, 1996).
- Dawood, N. J. *The Koran* (London: Penguin Books, 1999).
- Pickthall, Mohammed M. *The Meaning of the Glorious Koran* (Kuwait: Dar al-Islamiyya).
- Rodwell, J. M. *The Koran* (North Clarendon, Vermont: Tuttle Publishing, 1994).

Translating the Koran and other Dr. Bill Warner's books from English to other languages

When translating Dr. Bill Warner's books, CSPI primarily uses the respective authoritative Koran translations. In cases where there are no authoritative translations or the existing translations differ significantly from the quotations used by Dr. Warner (e.g. they substantially soften the violence of the text), the translation follows the English original used by Dr. Warner.

BIBLIOGRAPHY

Ali, Maulana Muhammad. *Holy Koran*. Columbus, Ohio: Ahmadiyyah Anjuman Ishaat Islam, 1998.

Arberry, A. J. *The Koran Interpreted*. New York: Touchstone, 1996.

Dawood, N. J. *The Koran*. London: Penguin Books, 1999.

Fishbone, Michael. *The History of al-Tabari VIII The Victory of Islam*. New York: The State University of New York Press, 1987.

Guillaume, A. *The Life of Muhammad* (a translation of Ishaq's *Sirat Rasul Allah*). Karachi: Oxford University Press, 1967.

Khan, Muhammad M. *The Translation of the Meanings of Sahih Al-Bukhari: Arabic-English*. Riyadh: Darussalam, 1997.

McDonald, M.V., and W. Montgomery Watt. *The History of al-Tabari, vol. VII, The Foundation of the Community*. New York: The State University of New York Press, 1987.

Muir, Sir William. *Life of Mohammed*. New York: AMS Press, 1975.

Pickthall, Mohammed M. *The Meaning of the Glorious Koran*. Kuwait: Dar al-Islamiyya.

Poonawala, Ismail K. *The History of al-Tabari, vol. IX, The Last Years of the Prophet*. New York: The State University of New York Press, 1987.

Robinson, Neal. *Discovering the Koran*. London: SCM Press, 1996.

Rodwell, J. M. *The Koran*, North Clarendon, VT: Tuttle Publishing, 1994.

Warraq, Ibn. *What the Koran Really Says*. Amherst, NY: Prometheus Books, 2002.

Watt, W. Montgomery, and Richard Bell. *Introduction to the Quran*. Edinburgh: Edinburgh University Press, 1970.

Watt, W. Montgomery, and M.V. McDonald. *The History of al-Tabari, vol. VI, Muhammad at Mecca*. New York: The State University of New York Press, 1987.

ABOUT THE AUTHOR

Dr. Bill Warner had a life-long interest in religions, including Islam, and their effects on history and civilizations. After the 9/11 New York jihad attacks, he began working to make the Islamic political doctrine, which impacts non-Muslims, available to the average person.

Dr. Warner's training in scientific theory and mathematics shaped how he analyzed the ideology of Islam. Realizing that the Islamic foundational texts were difficult to read and comprehend, he set out to organize them so they could be easily understood. As he analyzed the Islamic texts, it became clear that the Islamic civilization of culture, religion and politics, based on a theocracy, is not constructed on the same civilizational principles as the rest of the world. Simple statistical methods revealed that dualism and submission were the foundational principles of Islamic doctrine.

Dr. Warner founded the Center for the Study of Political Islam (CSPI) to further the study of political Islam and its ramifications for Western Civilization. He has written over a dozen books that teach about political Islam and make the Islamic doctrine understandable. He also developed the first self-study course on political Islam.

Dr. Bill Warner holds a Ph.D. in physics and applied mathematics from North Carolina State University. He has held positions as a research scientist, business owner and college professor.

AFTERWORD

CENTER FOR THE STUDY OF POLITICAL ISLAM
INTERNATIONAL (CSPII)

Center for the Study of Political Islam (CSPI) is an educational organization dedicated to enlightening the general public about the doctrine of political Islam based on the works of Dr. Bill Warner.

CSPI International (CSPII) is the volunteer-based, non-profit educational organization of CSPI that translates and publishes books, provides trainings and lectures, does research, and offers the ability to connect with like-minded people world-wide who want to be active. If interested in joining, go to www.cspii.org.

Islam is an ideology, a complete civilization, with a culture, a religion and a political or legal system. It is the political system that is of concern, for that is the part that defines the role of the non-Muslim or Kafir.

CSPII is interested only in the ideology of political Islam, and not with the religion or its members. Our organization values rational thought and debate about political ideas. The world has a new tool to deal with Islam – fact based reasoning and a knowledgeable active community.

If you like our work and agree that it is important to spread the information about political Islam, you can help in several ways:

- Share the information with your family, friends, classmates, and colleagues.
- Start talking about Islam using the CSPI method. Train others to do the same.
- Support us with your time by volunteering for CSPII projects.
- Join us in our activities, such as translating, research, publishing, graphics, legal services, financial services, administration and many more.

Visit www.cspii.org/support-us. Thank you.

CSPI is an educational organization dedicated to the understanding of Islamic politics

Factual books that provide an overview of political Islam and its effect on the Western world by using a method that relies on Islam's original foundational texts.

Level 1: For Beginners

A Taste of Islam

Level 2: Special Topics

Applied doctrine to specific topics of interest

Self Study Course on Political Islam

These 3 books will end your confusion about Islam